They Can't Go Home Again

THEY CAN'T
GO HOME
AGAIN

The Story of
America's Political Refugees

Richard L. Killmer
Robert S. Lecky
Debrah S. Wiley

With an introduction by
the Honorable Edward I. Koch

A Pilgrim Press Book
Philadelphia

The article from *The New York Times*, Sunday, August 23, 1970, on page 106, is reprinted by permission of the Associated Press.

CONTENTS

Introduction by the Honorable Edward I. Koch   1

Preface   7

Chapter 1.   And So They Left   9

Chapter 2.   They Can't Go Home Again   17

Chapter 3.   Kitchener and Waterloo   39

Chapter 4.   Fathers and the Fatherland   51

Chapter 5.   The Eagle Scout   61

Chapter 6.   The Pioneer   69

Chapter 7.   The Clinic   77

Chapter 8.   The Larger Picture   83

Chapter 9.   Epilogue: A Man Without a Country   105

Appendix A.   The Number of U.S. Draft Age
                        Emigrants in Canada   109

Appendix B.   Aid Centers in Canada   115

They Can't Go Home Again

INTRODUCTION

On December 29, 1969 I went to Canada. I did so at the urging and request of several constituents who called and wrote to tell me that their sons are now living in Canada. Their sons were not ordinary emigrants, but had gone to Canada to avoid the draft. I read in 1968 a *New York Times* article that estimated that there were about 5,000 young Americans who had undertaken a similar exile. And so, I decided to go and see for myself what the situation actually was. I contacted Clergy and Laymen Concerned About Vietnam (CALCAV) which I knew had undertaken a ministry to these young men. The Rev. Richard Killmer of CALCAV arranged my visit.

The trip by necessity was brief. But in my two day visit, Rich Killmer opened to me the feelings, frustrations, concerns, and hopes of the young men who had come to Canada—many with wives and children—to find a new way of life. And now, in "They Can't Go Home Again," Rich Killmer, Robert Lecky, and Debrah Wiley bring to the American people who cannot make a trip to Canada, this same perspective on what the young emigrants are thinking, how they have adjusted to their new jobs and country, and even how they feel about some day returning to the United States.

My visit began in Toronto where I met with five members of

the Canadian Parliament for lunch. I learned that the Canadians are delighted with this immigration of American youth into their country.

Earlier in 1969 there had been a Parliamentary hassle over whether Canadian immigration inspectors at the border could discriminate against deserters from the American Army as distinguished from draft evaders. But, with the support of Prime Minister Trudeau, Canadian Minister of Immigration and Manpower Allan MacEachen issued a statement in Parliament on May 22, 1969 clarifying the government's policy that desertion was not to be considered a bar to landed immigrant status.

During our lunch with the Members of Parliament, one of the guests, an American emigre now a draft resistance counselor pointed out that the government's policy was not being uniformly followed at all border points. One of the Canadian M.P.s at the luncheon was chairman of the committee having jurisdiction of border stations and was very distressed to hear such a report. He requested specifics and promised to follow up to insure that the laws and regulations would be uniformly applied. While it is generally believed that approximately 30,000 draft age Americans have emigrated to Canada since 1966, another Member of Parliament told me that he estimated the friendly "invasion" of Americans from the south to be 60,000 and that perhaps 140,000 more might immigrate before the war in Vietnam is concluded. I was staggered by the dimensions of his forecast, but it was clear to me that aside from the Canadian interest in benefiting from the talents and skills of these young immigrants, they enjoy the idea of tweaking the nose of the superpower to the south whose wealth and media so often intrude and threaten to dominate Canadian business and culture.

In Toronto that afternoon I went to a Canadian draft resistance reception and counseling center and talked with William Spira, a Canadian who had himself left Hungary as a refugee. He told me he was devoting every waking minute of the day to a very successful refugee operation. I asked him if I could sit in on one of the interviews. The interviewee was a young woman who identified herself as a Canadian and the wife of a young American who was still in the United States. They lived in a Midwestern city and he is in the last year at the university. He was expecting his induction notice momentarily and she was there in Toronto to make arrangements for their departure from the United States. She made it clear that they wanted to hold out as long as possible so that they could get their college degrees. Spira assured her that entry was easy and ticked off the various documents they should have with them, long in advance, so that they could leave on a moment's notice.

She said to him, "When we come up, can we bring our belongings in the car?"

He responded, "No, because technically you are coming here as tourists and tourists don't load their cars with household furniture."

Then she asked, "Can we at least bring the TV with us?"

She also explained that they had a dog. Spira told her, "You bring with you your toothbrush and your dog."

In the middle of the conversation, the young woman said to Spira, pointing at me, "Who's he?"

"It's alright, he is a friend," he told her.

She responded in a very cool voice, "I've heard that line before." And then in a much softer tone, "Are you the Congressman they are talking about?"

And I said, "Yes."

She then said to me, "You have got to do something. My husband does not want to go and I will not let him go to Vietnam to slaughter Vietnamese."

Spira said to me after she had left, "We get 40 a day now coming through and," he went on to say with a laugh, "four Ph.Ds came through today."

In leaving I went through the cellar office of four or five cramped rooms with people standing in line to be interviewed for immediate lodging assistance, and most important the information needed to quiet their nerves and assure them that at last they were safe.

I passed a young very well-dressed couple and the young man said to me, "Thank you for coming, Congressman Koch. I am one of your constituents." We shook hands and I left.

Next I flew to Ottawa and at about 8:00 P.M. I came to the home of Professor of English James Wilcox, who is an American emigre and who coordinates the counseling of draft resisters who come to Ottawa. He had brought together about 20 young men for me to meet and talk with. They were either draft resisters or deserters.

I inquired of these young men about their reasons for coming to Canada. "Was it only," I asked, "the war in Vietnam?" Almost all of them said that the war in Vietnam and the draft were the major reasons but not the only reasons; they were disillusioned with American society which they felt was hypocritical and intolerant. Those who were deserters mentioned Army and Marine brutality which they had suffered or seen. I asked whether they had as their goal some form of ultimate amnesty and I was surprised to learn that return to the United States was not their major concern. Most of them were intent upon making their careers and raising their families in Canada. A young man and his wife, both teachers from Nebraska, were very quick to say that if the war were over and amnesty were offered, they very much wanted to come back. Others said that what they wanted most of all was the opportunity some day to visit their families in the United States from whom they were separated. There were several infants in the room, and my whole feeling about those with whom I spoke was that they nourished no hatred for their country. Neither were they cowards—indeed, some of them have fought in Vietnam. They were intelligent young Americans seeking answers to questions which should bother every thoughtful individual and while they had taken a route different from that which most would take in responding to the problems besetting our country, they took it proudly. They came from every section of the United States, and of the 20 assembled, three were Jews and the other 17 were split almost evenly between the Protestant and Roman Catholic religions.

That night I stayed at the home of a young Canadian born couple. The wife is a counselor to newly arrived resisters and deserters. Her husband is a Canadian union organizer. Over tea and cookies, we talked a little.

"What does being an immigration counselor mean?" I asked.

She replied, "It means taking a frightened young American recently arrived in a strange country and providing him with friendships and contacts, and making it possible for him to lift his head without fear, and to find a place for him to live, and a job to hold and ultimately to help him become a Canadian citizen."

She told me that of all those she had counselled over the several years in which she has been involved only one had turned out bad. When placed with a minister for overnight lodging, he had stolen something. I asked, "What did you do under those circumstances?"

She said, "I reported it to the local police. We expect them to help us because we obey the law and therefore we have no hesitation in reporting when someone violates it."

The next morning I flew to Montreal on the final leg of my trip before returning home. Because the airport was far from the city and my time was short, I met with four deserters at a motel adjacent to the airport. One of them had been a journalist covering the war in Vietnam before his induction and was now writing a book on the draft resisters in Canada. Another was a young man who had sought conscientious objector status while serving in the Army, which was denied, according to him, because of his participation in various moratoriums and GI coffee house activities. The third had entered the Army for the express purpose of engaging in anti-war activities but had been discouraged by the opportunities offered. The last of the four had served in the Marine Corps for 3½ years.

Flying back to New York City in my comfortable Eastern Airlines' armchair, I found myself humming an old folk song and realized it was "Follow the Drinking Gourd," a folk song of the slaves in the old south which contained directions for them on how to use the "underground railroad." The drinking gourd was their description of the North Star and they were to follow it to freedom. Today there is a new underground railroad, and strange as it seems to many of us, for many young Americans the drinking gourd leads on to Canada.

Edward I. Koch
United States Congressman
from the 17th District, New York

PREFACE

The authors wish to express thanks and appreciation to those persons who made the book possible.

To the twenty resisters and deserters who agreed to extensive interviews for the book, we are grateful. Their names have been changed not at their request, but because we wished to avoid any more pain for them or their families. The Aid Centers throughout Canada and the Canadian Council of Churches, and concerned Canadians, were also helpful in arranging contacts and supplying information.

Two other persons did interviewing with the men. Father Redmond McGoldrick, S.J. spoke with Americans in Toronto; William McNeil, a student at the University of Chicago Divinity School interviewed deserters and resisters in British Columbia. We greatly appreciate their work.

Susan Felton, administrative assistant in the Emergency Ministry Concerning U.S. Draft-age Emigrants in Canada, did a great deal of research for the book. Elizabeth Stowe, a student at Pacific School of Religion, helped edit the book. For their energy and competence we are thankful.

A special word of thanks is due to Jack Biersdorf, executive director of the Department of Ministry, who has been colleague and friend to the three of us during this project.

To our families and friends who tolerated the confusion and frustration which book writing brings, we express our love and thanks.

Richard L. Killmer
Robert S. Lecky
Debrah S. Wiley

Veterans Day, 1970

chapter 1
AND
SO THEY LEFT

And so they left. Leigh maneuvered the white Chevrolet pick-up truck through the winding streets of the Los Angeles suburb and on to the freeway heading North. Joan, who was six months pregnant, had been warned by her doctor that long truck rides were not exactly conducive to healthy pregnancies. The Manns had therefore prepared for a longer trip that would be as relaxing and unhurried as possible.

Joan looked out the back window checking their belongings in the back of the truck. "I wish we could have found a covered van," she thought. "If it rains everything will be soaked; those cloth covers won't hold much moisture."

Leigh wasn't thinking about their furniture, nor about his driving nor about the California that was outside his window. His thoughts were on what would happen in three days and the meaning of that event for the rest of their lives.

A V.W. suddenly pulled into his lane and Leigh instantly put on the brake. The move made him conscious of his driving. He looked carefully at the freeway and at the houses which bordered it. "God, I'm never going to drive this freeway again. I'm never going to be able to come back to California."

His thoughts jumped quickly from one event to another as he tried to put together the reasons why this would be his last drive in his home state. Leigh remembered a number of conversations he had in high school—conversations about the war in Vietnam. Most of his friends thought it stupid, yet not stupid enough to refuse to fight in it.

During his freshman year at Stanford University, he had attended a major teach-in. He remembered agreeing with most of the speakers, listening very carefully to the arguments and the facts so that he would be able to argue well against the war.

His major in economics had helped him understand U.S. foreign policy and the role of foreign investments in that policy. Leigh concluded that the war in Vietnam was not just a bad mistake but was part of a foreign policy that was often destructive of Third World people.

During his senior year in college, he began to look at the Vietnam war as more than an intellectual problem. The draft, facing him immediately following graduation, pressed a sense of urgency upon him; his opinion about the war became, in a sense, "a matter of life and death." Even after graduation, though, Leigh had not come to any firm decision.

One month after his marriage to Joan that summer, Leigh received his induction order. The options—military service, Canada, or jail—were constantly on his mind. He was neither religious as defined by the selective service system nor an absolute pacifist, so conscientious objector status was not a possible alternative.

Before the day of his induction, Leigh had concluded that he would neither go into the military nor would he go to jail. Emigration to Canada, therefore, had to be his choice. Joan readily agreed, and they began to make plans. They talked with a number of persons who knew something about Canada and Canadian immigration law. From this information, Joan and Leigh decided that Calgary would be their new home.

Leigh clearly remembered the day he and Joan sat in his parents' living room telling them of their choice. He remembered the tension and the tears and the subsequent phone calls from every member of their families trying to dissuade them.

Only a week ago, an F.B.I. agent had visited him and asked

why he had not appeared for his induction. The agent said that Leigh would be given another chance—another induction notice. The Manns immediately hurried their plans for emigration.

"Love, do you know that I'll never drive this road again?"

"It's not very important, Leigh. There are roads in Canada you know."

They talked further about their sadness at being forced to leave and their worry about what would happen at the border.

The first night on the road they stayed with a close friend, Joseph, who had a cabin in the White Mountains of California. He had decided to take another course of action and was going to join the Army's Officer Candidate School. Joseph also hated the war and did not want to be in the military, but more important to him was freedom to travel throughout the world, including the United States. He could not accept the restrictions that emigrating to Canada would place on him.

The next two nights they camped in state parks in Idaho and Western Montana. The fourth night they stayed in a dreary little motel in Browning, Montana—seventy miles from the Canadian border. After a restless night, the morning finally arrived and they left the motel very early heading for the border.

When they arrived, they were met by the officer examining cars. When told that they wished to apply for landed immigrant status—the first step toward becoming Canadian citizens—he pointed to the small white house next to the border. They parked the car, entered the house, and told the man at the desk what they wanted. They were asked to sit while waiting for an immigration officer.

After half an hour, a young, nervous-looking officer invited them into his office. The officer looked at the Manns' application form and asked them questions, often looking in the several books on his desk after they answered. Seeing the puzzled looks on their faces, he told them that they were the first applicants he had processed.

When the interview was over, the officer informed them that he could not grant them landed immigrant status at that time, because they lacked the five hundred dollars in cash required for a couple applying to be landed. He suggested that they return to Browning and wait for money from home. Remembering the visit from the F.B.I., Leigh was reluctant to spend any time at all in the United States. He asked the officer if they might go on to Calgary as visitors to look for a job and wait for the money. The officer had not let them know whether or not they had obtained the necessary 50 out of a possible 100 points to become landed, but he had suggested that a job offer would be helpful. Leigh had known that a job offer would give him ten points toward the fifty he needed, but while still in California he had been too anxious about being arrested to make a preliminary trip to Calgary. He had wanted to enter Canada permanently when he went.

The official said that he wasn't sure if they could go through as visitors and looked through his books again. He left the room, apparently to speak with a senior immigration officer and returned saying that they could enter Canada as visitors.

Overjoyed, Leigh and Joan drove to Calgary, an expansive residential city. Knowing no one there, they felt lonely and lost in the jungle of streets lined with houses that seemed identical. Although the persons who had advised them about Canada had failed to mention the required $500, they had given the Manns a phone number of the Calgary Committee for War Immigrants— one of twenty Aid Centers throughout Canada. Leigh dialed the number, and an older woman answered the phone. Leigh explained who he was and their predicament. She invited them to come to her home.

"Welcome to Canada" was Mrs. Brookman's greeting as she opened her door. In the conversation that followed, Joan told Mrs. Brookman of her background. Mrs. Brookman asked some questions about the persons Joan knew in her home town and discovered that she had grown up with the mother of Joan's closest friend.

Mutual trust and respect developed quickly. Mrs. Brookman offered the Manns a room in her house until Leigh found a job.

Calgary has an expanding economy, and in 1969 jobs were not

difficult to find. Leigh applied at a large insurance company and was immediately hired as a salesman. Mrs. Brookman and the Committee loaned the Manns the five hundred dollars. With the money, the job, and more accurate and adequate advice on immigration than they had had when first leaving the U.S., Joan and Leigh headed back to the border one week after they had been in Calgary.

This time they were interviewed by the Chief Immigration Officer, a stern-looking man who looked them straight in the face and asked a great many questions. Under Canadian Immigration law, the officer has 15 points which he can give as he sees fit for personal assessment. Their interviewer was personally very concerned about the kind of people who wanted to live in Canada, wanting only those persons admitted who were sincerely committed to working and helping his nation.

The Manns were honest with him in their reasons for leaving the U.S. Leigh explained about his draft status and his refusal to fight in the war. Joan added that she already knew something of Canada's social, political, and economic problems. "Yet," she concluded, "Canada is a relatively young country and is attempting to solve its problems. I have a sense of future and hope for Canada which I no longer have for the United States."

The official responded to their sincerity, announcing that they had sufficient points and were now landed immigrants.

The Manns drove back to Calgary where they made permanent arrangements to live in a basement apartment, a housing arrangement common among young couples in Calgary. Leigh began to work at the insurance company. Three weeks later, the manager called him into the office and told Leigh that the home office of the company in New York had learned that he was a draft resister. They did not want to take the risk that there might be something illegal about hiring a resister, the manager said, and therefore he had been instructed to let Leigh go.

The manager expressed his anger at the interference of the home office in the affairs of his branch, to all intents and purposes a Canadian firm. He resented an American office telling him, a Canadian, what to do, and yet he had no choice. The manager recommended Leigh to another insurance agency with a home office in Toronto, and again he was hired immediately. A year after they had arrived in Calgary, Leigh switched to a job in managerial training.

He has spent a great deal of time with the Calgary Committee for War Immigrants advising other young men on immigration procedures, wanting to help others as he had been helped and concerned that these men become productive Canadians in their new country.

The Manns' child was born during their third month in Canada. With the baby almost a year old, Joan will go to the University of Calgary and complete her education.

The Manns are making it in their new country.

◆   ◆   ◆   ◆   ◆

Leigh Mann is one of some 30,000 draft age Americans who have emigrated since early 1965. On March 2nd of that year, the United States began on a sustained basis the bombing of logistical sites in Vietnam. By that date, there were 23,000 U.S. ground troops in Vietnam.

The war in Vietnam has produced resistance, rifts, and disjunctions within the society comparable only to those created by the American Revolution and the Civil War. Polls have indicated that almost one-half of all Americans believe that it was a mistake to be involved militarily in Vietnam, while the others believe not only that the war is necessary and right, but doubt the patriotism and loyalty of those who oppose it. This polarity has led even to violent confrontation. The clash between construction workers and peace groups in New York in the spring of 1970 exemplifies this national rift.

Young men face the war in a special way, for it is they who are drafted to fight. Any intellectual decision they make about the war has to be arrived at in the light of the draft, and the implications of their decisions may be immediately—and often dramatically—felt. Some men do choose to fight. There are others, though, that refuse.

Refusal to fight leads to several forms of resistance. Some men apply for exemptions and deferments in order not to be drafted. Others apply for classification as conscientious objectors to participation in all wars. During the first seven months of 1970 some 5,000 men were granted this status which requires two years of alternate civilian service in the nation's "health, safety, or interest."

Yet many men who apply are not granted the C.O. status. The law states that conscientious objectors must "by reason of religious training and belief be opposed to war in any form." The phrase "opposed to war in any form" is usually interpreted to mean opposition to participation in all wars—past, present, future. They have difficulty conjecturing what they would do in hypothetical wars. Their claim is that in conscience they cannot fight in the war they face. Some local draft boards are unwilling to give a man a conscientious objector status unless he is a member of a traditional peace church, such as the Mennonites, Society of Friends or The Church of the Brethren. The Supreme Court has decided in the Welch case (June 15, 1970) that men whose objection to war is based on grounds other than religious may also be entitled to a conscientious objector status. It has yet to be seen whether this will affect the actual practice of draft boards.

Other men say that they will have nothing to do with the war or with the draft that makes the war possible and refuse to be inducted into the Armed Services. In fiscal year 1970 there were 3,712 prosecutions for Selective Service violations. Many of these men and other resisters are opposed to conscription in principle, claiming that it is a form of involuntary servitude.

Some men who are already in the military find that their consciences prevent them from fighting in Southeast Asia. During fiscal 1967 there were 40,227 deserters—men who have been absent from the military without leave for thirty days or more. During fiscal 1970, there were 89,088 deserters.

Thirty thousand men have chosen to resist the war and the draft by leaving their nation. This book will examine this exodus and the reasons why this particular form of resistance has been chosen by such a large number of young men.

chapter 2
THEY CAN'T GO HOME AGAIN

EMIGRATION TO OTHER COUNTRIES

Deserters and resisters have emigrated to a number of countries and under a variety of circumstances. Until recently deserters were allowed in France, though they were never encouraged to immigrate; now residence permits are being denied. Several deserters have officially been granted residence in Denmark. In England it is estimated by the Union of American Exiles, a group aiding American draft age men, that there are 200 resisters and deserters in that country. Resisters are being granted work permits or student visas (which are good for one year and are renewable) and are not being forced to leave. Permanent residence status can be obtained after living in Britain for four years and citizenship after five.

Deserters, however, are not allowed visitor, work, or student permits. They are liable to prosecution by U.S. military authorities under the Visiting Forces Act of 1952, the British extension of the provision of the NATO treaty governing armed forces deserters. There is a campaign underway in Great Britain to obtain political refugee status for American deserters and resisters, thereby granting them protection against deportation to the U.S. Men are probably underground—in a country illegally—in other nations such as Japan.

The first deserter to emigrate to Sweden arrived in May 1967.

As of November 1970, approximately 500 deserters and draft resisters had asked the Swedish government for permission to remain there. Of these, most have been granted residence and work permits by the Immigration Department, a few have left Sweden before receiving permits, a very few cases have been denied, or are under consideration. About 25 men have deserted from Vietnam to Sweden, many coming via Japan and the Soviet Union. Permission to remain in Sweden has been granted for "humanitarian reasons." A deserter or resister who can document his situation has no trouble receiving a permit.

The Immigration Department has employed a special social worker to work with these men. In 1969 Mrs. Kristian Nystrom, who held the position at that time, indicated in a press conference a satisfactory rate of assimilation of these young Americans into Swedish life. At that time, she had contacted 294 deserters and resisters, of whom 104 were working, 103 attending Swedish language classes, 7 in folk high schools (preparatory schools for university work), 9 in adult high schools, 6 in vocational studies, while 16 were studying at the University of Stockholm and 14 others were attending special courses arranged by the National Market Labor Board.

The deserters and resisters in Sweden compose a heterogeneous group, ranging in age from 17 to 30, in education from seventh grade to completed university degrees in law, in military rank from private to captain. The average age is 20, and most are unmarried.

CANADA

Most draft resisters and deserters have chosen Canada as their new home. Geographical proximity is a major factor. Most young people do not have funds for overseas transportation, whereas it is possible to hitchhike to Canada, as many have done.

Furthermore, Canada has the image of a country with much land to explore and discover. It is a nation with frontiers yet to be pushed back. The economy is expanding, despite the high prices and high unemployment rate currently plagueing the nation. Great mineral and oil wealth abound, much of which remains untouched.

Yet the major reason for the large number of deserters and draft resisters emigrating to Canada is the openness of their immigration law. Under Canadian law, men who evade the draft or desert are free to enter Canada and to seek citizenship there—a fact generally known among young people. Canada does not bar these men from entering as visitors, nor from applying for landed immigrant status, the first step toward becoming a Canadian citizen. The extradition treaties between Canada and the U.S. do not include draft evaders or deserters, since Canada has no draft.

The official immigration policy of Canada does not discriminate against deserters and resisters. On May 22, 1969, Canadian Minister of Immigration and Manpower, Allan MacEachen, said: "An individual's status with regard to compulsory military service in his own country has no bearing upon his admissibility to Canada. Nor is he subject to removal from Canada because of unfulfilled military obligations in his own country."

The Pearson and Trudeau Governments have always had open stated policies toward American draft resisters. For example, on February 1, 1967, Prime Minister Pearson made clear his Government's willingness to accept applications from draft dodgers. John C. Munro, then Parliamentary Secretary to the Department of Manpower and Immigration, told the House of Commons on June 12 of the same year, that "an individual's status with regard to compulsory military service in his own country has no bearing upon his admissibility to Canada either as an immigrant or as a visitor." (James Wilcox, "They're Up Against the Canadian Border," *I Would Like to Dodge the Draft Dodgers But . . .* [Frank Epp, ed., Waterloo, Ontario and Winnipeg, Manitoba: Conrad Press, 1970], p. 51.)

This official policy has not always been closely adhered to in practice. During 1967, the Aid Centers (groups organized to help American draft age immigrants) in Ottawa, Montreal, Toronto and Vancouver had begun to collect a great deal of evidence that immigration officials were often treating draft resisters in a prejudicial manner that violated, in both letter and spirit, Canadian immigration law. (*Ibid.,* p. 50.)

In October of 1967, the Privy Council revised the immigration regulations. The Privy Council consists of the cabinet of the government and a few other officials who serve as an advisory body to the Prime Minister. Their orders usually become the law of the land. The revision attempted to give greater objectivity to the process by which an immigration officer judges the qualifications of individuals applying for admission to Canada. Persons were to be judged on a merit system of 100 points, of which 50 would be needed to become landed.

Points are given in the following categories:

1. Education and training—one point for each year of training, a maximum of 20 points.

2. Personal assessment—judged by the immigration officers at the interview, a maximum of 15 points.

3. Occupational demand—points given on the basis of the need for the skill the applicant possesses, a maximum of 15 points.

4. Occupational skill—points given on the degree of skill possessed by the applicant, a maximum of 10 points.

5. Age—10 points given if the applicant is between the age of 18 and 35, one point deducted for each year of age over 35.

6. Arranged employment—10 points if the applicant has arranged employment within Canada.

7. Knowledge of English and French—points given for various degree of fluency in these languages, maximum of 10 points.

8. Relatives in Canada—points given if the applicant has relatives in Canada who are unwilling or unable to *sponsor* or *nominate* him ("sponsor" and "nominate" refer to procedures which greatly reduce the number of points needed by the applicant), maximum of 5 points.

9. Employment opportunities in the area of destination—5 points given if the applicant is going to an area where there are great labor demands—fewer points if the demand is less.

A landed immigrant differs from a citizen only in that he may not vote in some elections, he is not eligible for certain government jobs, he cannot obtain a Canadian passport and he can be deported for certain fairly well-defined offenses. After five years as a landed immigrant, he is eligible for citizenship.

No changes were made in the prohibited class category in which certain persons (including criminals, persons known to use drugs—including marijuana, persons with certain mental or physical illnesses, and some others) are refused admission to Canada, no matter how many points they acquire.

Yet even with this attempt at fairness, there were still a rather large number of immigration officials who discriminated against American draft resisters. The Aid Centers continued to collect evidence of this discrimination, according to Dr. James Wilcox, a professor at Carleton University and the former director of Ottawa Assistance with Immigration and the Draft. (*Ibid.*)

In January, 1968, the practice of requiring proof of discharge from men in the military applying for landed immigrant status was eliminated for those applying at an internal immigration station. This meant that deserters applying from within Canada were not to be refused admission because of their military status. Deserters applying at border stations were still required to prove that they were discharged or were to be discharged.

On July 29, 1968, the office of the Minister of Immigration, Allan MacEachen, in the new government of Pierre Trudeau, issued a memo ending the practice of requiring proof of discharge at the border immigration stations. The practice was replaced by one which gave the power of discretion to immigration officers. Under this policy an immigration officer could either consider or disregard desertion as a factor when processing applicants for landed immigrant status.

The memo which was confidential went on to remind officers of section 32(4) of the Immigration Regulations—"if in his opinion there are good reasons why those norms (the point system) do not reflect the particular applicant's chances of establishing himself successfully in Canada," the applicant may be denied.

It then designated three reasons for such rejection: excessive financial debts, marital desertion and military desertion. (*Ibid.,* pp. 52-53.)

It became clear to those working in Aid Centers with Americans that discrimination against deserters was widespread. They found men with post-graduate degrees who had been refused landed immigrant status. Even in the Ottawa immigration office, which had a reputation for being fair, deserters' applications were delayed for at least three months without a decision, while other applicants knew their results within one week of their assessment. In a private interview, Mr. MacEachen conceded that since an overwhelming majority of immigration officers are former servicemen, the discretion given to them seemed unlikely to operate in the deserter's behalf. (*Ibid.,* p. 54.)

In December 1968 and January 1969, the three Aid Centers in Ottawa, Montreal, and Toronto held meetings to discuss what action should be taken to end the excessive discrimination against American resisters and deserters. The group decided that publicity and parliamentary lobbying were the tools available to them. Dr. Wilcox directed the lobbying campaign, while Bill Spira of the Toronto Anti-Draft Programme led the press campaign.

On February 8, William John Heintzelman, an "American deserter," applied for landed immigrant status—simultaneously at five stations. In each case, the man who was in reality a Canadian citizen had been turned down by immigration officials. All five officials told Mr. Heintzelman that he would not be allowed in Canada, and four of the men were sent back to the U.S. border with phone calls to American officials indicating that they were on their way.

When the five men told their story, the Canadian public, press, and many public figures were horrified at the disclosures of discrimination. The July 29 memo which seemed to sanction this discrimination was also released by Aid Centers, to the shock and dismay of press and public. (*Ibid.,* p. 52.)

The publicity continued into April and May. Press coverage emphasized the confusion in the Department of Immigration as one official denied discrimination and another defended immigration practice; the July 29, 1968 memo was similarly denied by one and defended by another. At the same time, the lobbying campaign among members of Parliament to end the de facto discrimination went well. Many members who had not been aware of the discrimination felt appalled that Canadian officials were engaged in such practices.

On May 22, 1969, Allan MacEachen announced in the House of Commons the government's decision to accord deserters the same treatment given to all applicants for immigration. The Aid Centers now report that the decision has been followed by most immigration officials, although some discrimination still exists. (*Ibid.*, p. 58.)

Many men who are avoiding or plan to avoid the draft are attending Canadian universities. While students, they hold a "Student Entry Certificate," good for one year and renewable. It is granted when an applicant has been accepted by a reputable university or college and has sufficient funds to pay for the necessary expenses. Once a man completes his education, he may apply for landed immigrant status.

THE NUMBER

According to Canadian immigration policy, no record is kept of the motivations for emigration or the military status of any particular group of immigrants. Therefore it is impossible to give an accurate figure of the number of American draft resisters and deserters in Canada. Taking into account the number of men in the draft age category who have received landed immigrant status, the number of men seen by the Aid Centers, the number of American students in Canada and an educated guess of the number of Americans illegally in Canada (remaining longer than the six months visitors are allowed without receiving a student permit or landed immigrant status), it is estimated that there are at least 30,000 draft age immigrants in Canada. (For a more complete description of the number question see Appendix A.)

There are two types of draft-age immigrants in Canada: deserters and draft resisters. Draft resisters (or draft dodgers—the term does not have the same negative connotations in Canada it has in the United States) are men who leave before or without accepting induction into the military—they are not yet members of the armed services. Deserters are members of the armed services who have left the military illegally.

There is a great need for more sociological analysis of this exodus, and of the backgrounds of the men who make this choice. The Canadian Council of Churches is currently conducting a sociological study of this phenomenon. However, the generalization can be made that most draft resisters are well educated, have often developed skills and come from middle and upper-middle class backgrounds. Deserters usually are, on the other hand, high school graduates or dropouts (many obtaining a Graduate Equivalency Degree in the military), and are from a working class background. (At the time of publication, about two thirds of the men emigrating to Canada are deserters.)

THEY CAN'T GO HOME AGAIN

Can these men ever return to the U.S. without being prosecuted? It depends on a number of factors.

The Selective Service Act states that any man who refuses to submit himself for induction into the U.S. military when called faces a maximum sentence of five years in prison, $10,000, or both. The average sentence for draft violations currently is about three years. The fine is rarely imposed. As previously stated, a man who is in Canada cannot be prosecuted for this violation in Canada nor will he be returned to the U.S. for prosecution.

1. A man who goes to Canada before being inducted and who *does not* receive an induction order, *may return* without any risk. For instance, if a man goes to Canada during the year his lottery number is to be considered but is not called, he can return without being prosecuted.

2. A man in Canada who renounces his citizenship *before* he

receives his induction order, should be classified IV-C—an alien —by his draft board. He cannot be inducted into the military if he is IV-C. If he should return to the U.S. and is not yet 26 years of age, he could be inducted. If he is 26 or older, he would not be liable for induction. However, a man who has renounced his U.S. citizenship would find it difficult if not impossible to obtain an immigrant's visa necessary to remain in the U.S. permanently, since he has left the country to evade military service. Even if he came in as a visitor, he could be excluded or deported as an "undesirable" draft evader.

The Canadian Aid Centers recommend that a man not renounce his U.S. citizenship, but instead wait the five year period to be naturalized (become a citizen). A man who has become a naturalized Canadian after waiting the five year period, however, would have the same difficulty returning to the U.S. as one who has renounced his citizenship.

3. A man who renounces his citizenship, or becomes a Canadian citizen *after* he has been ordered for induction or otherwise violates the Selective Service Act can still be prosecuted for his violation if he should return to the U.S.

If a man is not indicted for an offense within five years of the time he committed it, the statute of limitations ordinarily forbids his indictment and makes him safe from prosecution. A draft refuser who has left the country and later returned, however, might not be safe from prosecution even if the government had neglected to indict him within the five year period. If he had left the country after violating the draft law, he might be held to be a "fugitive from justice" (someone who has fled to avoid prosecution) to whom the statute of limitations does not apply. Thus, a draft refuser may be subject to prosecution if he should ever return to the United States, even if he has renounced American citizenship (after violating the Selective Service Act) or become a citizen of a foreign country and even if he was not indicted within five years of violating the law. *This means that most men in Canada who have violated the Selective Service Act cannot return to the United States without risk of prosecution.*

The military makes an administrative distinction between A.W.O.L.'s—absent without leave for less than thirty days—and deserters—absent without leave for thirty days or more. This is for administrative purposes only and does not have any judicial effect, i.e., a man who is declared a deserter administratively may be declared A.W.O.L. by a court-martial. Judicially, the distinction between an A.W.O.L. and a deserter is in intent. A man who in the view of a court-martial did not intend to return to the military can be punished as a deserter. A man whom a court-martial believes did intend to return is seen as an A.W.O.L. The maximum sentence an A.W.O.L. can receive is one year in the stockade and a Dishonorable Discharge (this sentence can be imposed on men who have been absent over thirty days). In most cases the maximum sentence a deserter can receive is five years and a Dishonorable Discharge.

Desertion is considered by U.S. authorities to be a continuing felony. A man who deserts is always considered a deserter, and hence could be prosecuted as such if he returns to the U.S. Renunciation of U.S. citizenship does not remove his liability of prosecution, and therefore it is *never possible for a deserter to return to the U.S. without the risk of facing five years in a military prison, unless an amnesty is declared by the Congress or the President for such offenses.*

THE AID CENTERS

Since late 1966-early 1967 Aid Centers responding to the needs of U.S. draft age immigrants have developed throughout Canada and now number about 20. Most were organized and manned by Canadians, but since that time many have been operated by deserters and resisters themselves. All centers work on a shoestring budget and full-time staff receive very low pay (varying from $15-$50 a week). Besides those Canadians who organized the Aid Centers, many other Canadians support the groups and directly aid the men.

Though the Aid Centers understand their tasks differently and operate according to distinctive styles, there are certain tasks they all perform.

MEETING THE IMMEDIATE NEEDS

Most deserters and resisters coming to Canada know no one. They do not even know where they will stay. Deserters usually have made no plans at all since their moves were made hurriedly and secretly. The men therefore need housing, food and sometimes even clothing. A man deserting from Ft. Hood, Texas does not usually have the proper clothes for a Canadian winter.

All Aid Centers have a housing list with the names of persons who are willing to house Americans. Quakers, members of other churches and persons sympathetic to the immigrant's plight have made rooms available without charge, often offering food as well. Some free food programs in large cities have offered their services to Americans; one Anglican church in Toronto, for example, has fed many deserters and resisters.

Some Aid Centers provide housing as the crux of their program. The Vancouver Unitarian Committee to Aid War Objectors (which has since merged with the Vancouver Committee to Aid War Objectors) operated on the belief that to match the American with the "right" person offering housing was imperative. Occupational and sociological factors, religious background, and, where possible, personality characteristics were considered in making that choice. The Canadian with whom the young man stayed might help him find a job and begin the process of assimilation.

The persons offering housing sometimes help the man work through an initial emotional trauma. In Edmonton, a young New Zealand couple kept a deserter in their home for over three months. At first the man was moody and restless, yet seemed to be unable or unwilling to find a job and obtain landed immigrant status. The couple supported him as he tried to make sense of his action and discover how he would live in his new country. After three months, the man found his own housing, obtained a job, and is now a landed immigrant.

PROVIDING JOB COUNSELING

Canada is currently facing a very high unemployment rate. The national average is 6.7 percent (August 1970). The average in British Columbia is 10.1 percent, while in Quebec it is 8.9 percent (July 1970). This means that many Canadians have lost their jobs and are out of work. Some work in situations which do not fully utilize educational or job experience; several young Canadian women who have recently graduated from college in Saskatchewan were found working in a car wash because nothing else is available. Obviously it is very difficult for immigrants to find jobs under those conditions. While skilled and educated men can take their places in the competition for jobs, those lacking skills, have a very difficult time.

Most Aid Centers attempt to provide jobs or job leads to the newly arrived immigrants. Some employers have offered work in the past and these are usually asked first. The large Aid Centers —Vancouver, Toronto, Ottawa and Montreal—have full-time job counselors. The counselor in Vancouver has had manpower and personnel experience. The job counselor in Ottawa has found work for two-thirds of the men he sees—an incredible record. He describes his work as "finding work mostly with prejudiced employers for mostly unskilled fellows in a very depressed job market." (Bob Neufeld, "They Are Coming to Our Chapel Looking for Jobs," *I Would Like to Dodge the Draft Dodgers But . . .,* p. 84.)

IMMIGRATION COUNSELING

About five years ago, the predecessor of the Vancouver Committee prepared a pamphlet on immigrating to Canada. This along with the *Manual for Draft-Age Immigrants to Canada* prepared by the Toronto Anti-Draft Programme, has been used by thousands of potential emigrants and those in the United States who try to help them.

But many men enter Canada ignorant of the point system and

other aspects of Canadian immigration law. Some bring the documents they need with them—birth certificates, school transcripts, job references, and so on. But most need help in knowing which to get and in some cases how to get them. When parents are unwilling to help, securing documents may be especially difficult.

Applying for landed immigrant status can be difficult and dangerous. Most applications are made at the border, even by men who have been in Canada as visitors, since ten possible points for a job offer are only credited toward the applicant's score in an application made at a border immigration station. The danger for deserters and men who have received induction notices is that of arrest by U.S. officials. Difficulties arise because of the possibilities of discrimination or other uncontrollable problems in the interview. And there is always the risk of being turned down. The Aid Centers try to inform men about these possible dangers and problems, what they are likely to expect, and to help with the logistics of getting men to the border.

ASSIMILATION

Moving is usually a difficult step. In particular, putting down roots in a strange place can be frightening. Even with the similarities between Canada and the United States, moving from one to the other can be especially hard.

Aid Centers have developed ways to enable men to become a part of their new country as quickly as possible, speeding assimilation through the introduction of Americans to Canadians. This happens in a variety of ways. Housing is one means to aid assimilation. Contacts made through jobs, churches, and other organizations are invaluable. The Ottawa center supports a coffee house. One of the Toronto groups, The Hall, has a reception center that not only attempts to relieve the anxiety of the immigrant, but is able to refer men to agencies or organizations that can meet their needs or provide activities in which they are interested.

Some Aid Centers have encouraged American exile communities to form. Yet there have been differences of opinion on their value. Those persons who espouse them feel that they facilitate the necessary process of self-examination that a man must go through before becoming a part of Canadian society, while those who find them counterproductive base their position on two points. First, they believe that the way to become a Canadian is to live and work with Canadians, rather than fellow Americans, and second, they feel that American exile communities threaten or anger many Canadians, increasing the difficulty of eventual assimilation.

A small minority of the Aid Centers are highly political, attempting to assimilate young men by involvement in new left politics. For some men political activity can be a way of clarifying their own act. Also, the camaraderie which is frequently characteristic of political activity can be helpful to men who face a new country alone.

In Montreal, where French language and culture add to the difficulties of assimilation, there is the most political activity. During Memorial Day 1970, a pan-Canadian conference was held there, at which most of the Aid Centers were represented. The purpose of the meeting was to discuss common problems, share ideas, and discuss the possibilities of working more closely. Tom Hayden, a founder of Students for a Democratic Society and a member of the Conspiracy 7, and Carl Oglesby, also a founder of S.D.S., spoke. Both speakers emphasized the need for persons to stay in the United States and work for change there.

Many persons attending the conference, including some leaders of Aid Centers, were impressed. A few persons are therefore telling men, especially draft resisters, to go back to the States and work for change there. While this may have some effect on the exodus, it most likely will be very minimal. Even in Montreal, a minority of the deserters and resisters are political activists.

One area of increasing concern for Aid Centers is the number of men who cannot be landed and are becoming a part of the Canadian underground. The underground is closely related to the hippie and heavy drug scene. Since some of these men may have problems in their emotional health as well, their difficulties can be enormously complex. The Aid Centers, operating on their present slim budgets, are unable to provide the kinds of specialized help required. The problem is compounded by the fact that some of the press has generalized the activities and problems of this very visible minority to apply to all resisters and deserters, although these men are only a small minority.

THE PARENTS OF EMIGRANTS

Many parents of the young men who emigrate to Canada and elsewhere are hostile to their sons' act, viewing military service as an honorable obligation. Often fathers have fought in previous wars and are proud of their service record. Even more important, most of these parents live in an environment which shares and reinforces this understanding of military service and obligation. Local young men seem to enlist for service and submit to orders to go to Vietnam without resistance.

Parents tend to view their resisting son as a disgrace. To hide this disgrace they will not tell their friends and relatives, nor will many religious families even tell their clergyman. Instead, to hide their shame and prevent ostracism, they will deliberately isolate themselves. One pastor in Maryland has ministered to three such sets of parents after the sons informed him they were in Canada; the parents had been too ashamed to confide in him their sorrow and anxiety.

The following excerpt of a letter sent by one emigrant's mother to her son expresses even in its extreme statements the depth of fear and anxiety experienced:

"What can I say to a son who has become a deserter and traitor to his country, family and friends? You know that is what you are. You really had us proud of you and now you ask to be referred to as a man. You must be kidding. A man is not a sniveling coward who has to run away from any form of authority or discipline just because it is temporarily inconvenient. You must really be a feather in the cap of your Godless communist friends.

L_____ especially, since he is probably the one who convinced you that their way of life is all peaches and cream. You know you were always a sucker for the easy way out. Now you have decided to live with the scum of the U.S. and probably other countries. The 'Draft program' set-up is nothing but a sham and you know it deep in your heart. Maybe things aren't perfect here but at least we have tried to change it through due process of law. Look at that 'peace sign' ring you are wearing. What peace has it brought you? Everywhere it is held up as a symbol, there is violence—not love. In the past few days there has been testimony given that *all* the so-called peace movements in the country are communist controlled.

"You claim to love us and miss us. I don't think you are capable of real love for anyone or you wouldn't have done this. You say you hope you don't hurt us too much. Well let me tell you something, it would have been more merciful if you had killed all of us before you left. You didn't have to watch your brother cry and cry, your grandma and Aunt D_____ get sick, as well as putting Dr. S_____ down in his chair. He doesn't know where you are as yet, but you see, he has both M_____ and me under his care. M_____ has been seriously ill ever since you left and it looks as if he has to go to the hospital for an operation. As for me, I am on the verge of being committed to Danville. Nice thoughts, aren't they? No, you didn't hurt us—you killed us. But I am sure you aren't bothered.

"You know G_____, I carried a child for 9 months only to have it die, then I sat for a year and watched your sister slowly die, day by day, and fighting every day of it for her. Now it seems I have been watching you die too. The only difference is, the funeral mass will last for the rest of our lives.

"The only help we will give you are our prayers. I would never ask anyone for letters of recommendation for such an irresponsible act. As for a birth certificate, that will stay where it is. You will have to make up your mind. Search your heart and if you decide to come back, all you have to do is write or call. This is the only time you will hear from us. Your decision will affect your brothers' lives also. They will never be able to get any kind of a job where security is involved, because there will always be doubt.

"You have taught us a lesson though. Don't ever be too happy or proud and brag about any of your children because you get kicked right in the teeth. You have hurt your father so deeply, because he thought you two were really close together after all these years. I hope you can walk with your head in the air.

"Hoping to hear from you before the end of the month."

Obviously reactions such as this can hurt the emigrant. The decision to leave is a very difficult one to make, often causing guilt and anguish, and is very often frightening. Such a response from parents reinforces the negative feelings, making life much more difficult.

Yet parents experience ambivalence. While they may feel shame, because of their love, or disgrace, most feel terribly cut off from their son and have concern for his well-being.

These tensions are resolved in a number of ways. There are parents who will not open their son's mail, refuse to talk to him on the telephone, send angry letters and in some cases disown him. There are also those who will not talk about their son's location, will lie if the question is raised, and feel great shame, but do communicate with their son and do help him by locating important documents which he may need to become landed and by sending money.

Some parents are supportive of their son's act; they may conclude that, in a similar situation, they would make a similar choice. These parents are also in need of support, for in addition to worrying about their son in a strange land and about his future, they may feel particularly isolated in American society.

Most parents know little about the facts of their son's legal status or the immigration policies of Canada. Frequently unaware of the size of the exodus, some parents have thought that their son was one of only a few draft resisters or deserters in Canada.

Parents sometimes bear a particular burden at home with respect to legal authorities. It has been reported that the F.B.I. has visited parents of deserters and resisters. They have been known to harass them, sometimes entering the parents' home without a search warrant or telling the parents of their legal rights. A black mother in Detroit with speech and hearing difficulties was visited by the F.B.I. four times. In none of the visits did the F.B.I. show her a search warrant. In a harsh manner, including obscenities, they asked her the whereabouts of her son, a deserter. They visited her neighbors and harassed one who had severe emotional problems. Parents are not required to say anything without a lawyer present, but they do not always realize this.

The F.B.I. has been reported to have given out false information to parents, claiming that their son can be extradited, or that they or the Royal Canadian Mounted Police can bring emigrants back to the U.S. for prosecution. As previously stated, extradition treaties with Canada do not cover these acts, and the F.B.I. has no jurisdiction in Canada. In only one known case has the R.C.M.P. delivered men to U.S. authorities, and in that case a hearing was called to determine the legality of this act of the R.C.M.P.

THE CHURCH RESPONDS

On December 2, 1969, representatives of the Canadian and the American religious community met in Windsor, Ontario with draft resisters and deserters in Canada to learn about the situation and to discover what the response of the churches and synagogues would be. After the consultation, a report was issued to the General Assembly of the National Council of Churches which was meeting in Detroit. The General Assembly received the report and adopted guidelines for action. These were that the National Council of Churches:

1. Requests the Canadian Council of Churches to establish an instrumentality for receiving and distributing funds to Aid Centers according to criteria they establish.

2. Endorses a pastoral ministry to these refugees and to their wives and children.

3. Agrees to cooperate with member communions to establish a ministry to the parents of the young men who have emigrated.

4. Requests the appropriate bodies within member communions to make special efforts to bring to the attention of the military chaplains the special needs and circumstances of those who report indignities, violations of due process or civil rights, or who struggle with problems of conscience arising from the war.

5. Requests the Division of Inter-Church Aid, Refugee and World Services of the World Council of Churches to study the needs of these American refugees in Canada and to consider supporting the Canadian churches in this pastoral ministry.

The Canadian Council of Churches currently makes grants to ten of the Aid Centers through funds they have received from individuals and churches. In addition, the Council, national Canadian church bodies, local churches and other organizations are concerned with and in the process of devising programs specifically intended to respond to the emotional needs of all American draft age immigrants.

The Emergency Ministry Concerning U.S. Draft Age Emigrants in Canada was established in February, 1970 in order to fulfill guidelines approved by the General Assembly of the National Council of Churches in December, 1969. The tasks of the Emergency Ministry are five-fold:

1. The Ministry is to establish means to encourage and support pastors and rabbis performing the pastoral task with the parents of men who emigrate.

2. The Ministry will perform a communication task. The Canadian Council of Churches and the National Council of Churches will need specific kinds of information to carry out their ministries as effectively as possible.

3. The Ministry will encourage the American religious community to discover together what it can learn from the experiences of the deserters and resisters. It will also attempt to assure that the motivations of these young men be reported and the life they face in Canada be described to the American public.

4. The Ministry will enter into dialogue with military chap-

lains to discover what can be done to minister more effectively to
G.I.'s who report indignities or who struggle with problems of
conscience.

5. The Ministry will attempt to respond to young men who
struggle with problem of conscience posed by the Selective Service System or military service, by cooperating with related denominations to discover how draft and military counseling services
might be increased and improved.

By October 1970 the ministry to parents had been operating on
a regular basis for about three months. During that period the
families of 200 resisters and deserters had been visited.

At the November 1970 meeting of the Division of Interchurch
Aid, Refugee and World Service of the World Council of
Churches (DICARWS), it was agreed that an appeal should go
to all member churches for funds to help the Canadian Council
of Churches meet the needs of the American draft age immigrants in Canada. The funds and the appeal were to be handled
through the refugee department of DICARWS.

chapter 3
KITCHENER AND WATERLOO

Deserters and resisters are not easy to seek out in Kitchener-Waterloo, twin cities 70 miles west of Toronto with a combined population of 105,000. Although over 150 men have settled there, with their wives and girl friends, there is no hostel or center. Instead, the emigrants are scattered through the city: living in attractive apartments, working alongside Canadians, and in some cases marrying Canadians. Assimilation into the dominant middle class prevails in K-W: most men come to K-W because they want to assimilate into that environment, and they are encouraged to become a part of the community.

Although deserters and resisters can assimilate into the dominant society in the larger cities of Toronto, Montreal, and Vancouver, other life styles are also easily accessible there. There are American exile communities, which some believe prevent assimilation into the Canadian mainstream. There are also opportunities for anti-American politics, and this too tends to create a subculture, alien from the dominant culture. Likewise, young men in the drug scene are not part of the prevailing life style of Canada.

Men who wish to become a part of an American community, who are seeking fellow activists to support their political views and actions, or who wish to live in a drug subculture never come to K-W or leave soon after arrival. The speed with which young men and couples settle in the city and assimilate into community life can be attributed to several factors.

The deserter or resister who leaves for Canada without prior contacts or information most often heads for one of the larger, better-known cities. To know about K-W he has most likely heard about the area from a friend or a friend's friend and is aware of the feasible life styles in the community.

When he arrives and calls the local aid group, he receives immediate personal attention from one of three Canadians—two professors and a graduate student at the local university. Although K-W receives from five to nineteen men in any one week, the numbers at no time approach those handled by the aid groups in the larger cities; therefore this personal attention is possible. It can be crucial in the assimilation of the young man in a strange country with little money, no place to stay, and no idea where to begin to seek a job.

The emigrant can find initial housing with one of seventy families, both American and Canadian, who have opened their doors to deserters and resisters while they look for employment and apartments. This setup not only fulfills a man's physical needs but also serves to introduce him to the community and provide much needed support during his first days in Canada.

About half of the men who have come to K-W are students at the University of Waterloo or Waterloo Lutheran University, furthering not only their education but their assimilation into the community life.

Some of the deserters and resisters have been effective in reaching the community through speaking to church groups, high school, college, and university classes, and interested people in general. Together with the effort made by most K-W immigrants to become part of the community, these talks have created a noticeably better understanding among their Canadian neighbors of the moral issues surrounding the men's move and has brought forth offers of temporary housing and money to help the immigrants while they get settled and to meet emergency needs.

Assimilation into the Kitchener-Waterloo community is relatively easier to observe and analyze than assimilation in one of the larger cities—just as a movement of people to Cedar Rapids, Iowa could be more easily studied than one to Boston or New York. Immigration in K-W is facilitated by the large number of concerned individuals, the flexible and practical manner in which deserters and resisters are given assistance, and, perhaps most important, the desire of the men themselves to settle into Canadian life.

There is, however, variety in this process. A new living situation may be adjusted to only over time. The physical indications of settling—a job, an apartment—do not necessarily mean that an individual has assimilated. Neither is involvement in community affairs a decisive index; some people never participate in such activities, no matter where they live. The degree to which an individual feels himself a party of the community varies.

Steve and Sherry, a quiet, close-knit couple, settled in a small community outside of Kitchener, exemplify many aspects of assimilation. At age 25, they seem extremely established: Steve supervising landscaping at the University, Sherry sewing clothes for a boutique while awaiting the birth of twins. Says Steve: "We are doing the best we can in the environment that we're in. It's kind of false to try to save Canada from the United States. It's just the wrong position. We're trying to be as good a couple as we can in our situation and trying to help the people that we're closest to."

Both Steve and Sherry are reflective individuals. Concerned with living their convictions daily, they are oriented toward living as sensitive human beings in an often insensitive world, rather than toward solving world problems. They enjoy the quietness of their new community, wanting neither a lively social life nor involvement in community organizations. They have helped deserters and resisters with temporary housing, friendship, and whatever other aid they can give to recently arrived men. Although the first months were lonely, friendships are now established, and the couple look forward to their future in Ontario.

Steve grew up ". . . in a small town of 16,000 well-to-do citizens. They prided themselves with having no blacks." Early in college he became involved in the civil rights movement, but "when I was in college I spent most of my time doing the normal things—I joined a fraternity—a real college Joe." Steve couldn't settle, however, for the conservative pro-war sentiments of most of his classmates. "I went through quite a nasty process of self-identification, and it was on the basis of some of my results that I realized I was a pacifist. It wasn't just the Vietnam war, but warfare in general." Bob Dylan, the early folk-rock prophet and a classmate of Steve's, influenced his thought. His application for conscientious objector classification was rejected by his local draft board and by the state appeal board; since Steve had quit school, he received an induction notice soon after.

The choice of jail or emigration remained. "I could only see jail as ruining my life or any hopes of being a decent person. So I thought I would come to Canada to be a good Canadian and be able just to live, to work, to go to school when I can, raise a family."

Steve and Sherry visited Toronto to get information on becoming landed before making their final decision. Both sets of parents were sympathetic, but Steve's parents have not told neighbors of their emigration; his father feels that his business life might be jeopardized if the community knew. Steve, an only child, is sorry that he had to hurt his parents: "You don't want to hurt your parents. Obviously you hurt them. We're going to have children and they aren't going to have the normal grandparent role. It bothers me that it hurts. I can say, though, that I would have hurt them more if I had gone into the army—I would have hurt them more if I had gone into prison."

Steve feels ". . . the only thing you do when you come to Canada is you take away the immediate problem of going into the army which is a corrupt institution." Beyond that, he feels that he will have the same personal problems in Canada—or wherever he lives: problems of dealing with the conflicts of life as a pacifist. Beyond the elimination of the immediate question of the draft, however, Steve is freed to plan his life without the necessity of working within the framework of selective service laws. Even should amnesty be granted, Sherry and Steve plan to remain in Canada. Their primary feeling for the United States is one not of bitterness but of sorrow: "I feel sorry for the nation. With that much technology and resources, it has such a good chance of providing a decent standard of living for its own citizens and others. But with its messed up priorities, these capabilities are grossly misused. I just don't know how it could be so terrible—and it is terrible."

◆   ◆   ◆   ◆   ◆

Joe and a fellow Marine deserted to Canada on July 4th, completely fed up with the United States. "I was brought up with the American dream and all that—my family is the good, loyal-type, pro-American." Like other young Americans, however, he had felt increasingly bombarded with awareness of the problems in American society: "When I found that America wasn't all I had been told, I became angry. In 1963, during the civil rights movement I began to realize—at first I had thought it was just all those crazy people in the South. . . . For a couple of years I have been really nervous about the whole situation, worrying about the draft, the Vietnam war, pollution, the blacks, the cops killing another brother—everything. Just one thing after another. . . . It got so bad I couldn't even communicate with the people because there was so much hate." In the face of the urgency to do something about these problems, Joe also felt the inability to produce any needed change.

When in college, Joe was involved in draft counseling and moratorium activities; these provided an outlet for his hostilities and "if the draft hadn't gotten me, maybe I could have done some good." But he dropped out of school, and so had a choice of enlisting or being drafted. He decided to enlist in the Marines, "so I could see what it was really like." The service turned out to be worse than he had expected; his attempt to organize for servicemen's rights was almost impossible in the Marines, largely a voluntary force. When he finally couldn't take it anymore, Joe left.

In Canada, he feels that he can relax and live without the burdens he had felt in the U.S. While getting a job, he stayed with a Canadian professor in K-W. He plans to work for a year, save some money and then travel in western Canada and maybe Europe, then take some university courses. Eventually he thinks he may buy some land and build a small house. Joe expects to participate in Canadian politics, for he does not view the issues as insurmountable, as in the U.S. His plans, spoken of during his first weeks in Canada, could easily change, but they exhibit Joe's new feelings of freedom—his escape from the pressures of his former country.

◆   ◆   ◆   ◆   ◆

Tom, a physics major, recently graduated from Washington University in St. Louis, felt similar pressures. Because he transferred and took five years to complete his undergraduate degree, he lost his student deferment. In order to be able to finish, he spent a lot of time trying to regain the 2-S classification, making appeals and personal appearances before various selective service boards.

When graduate deferments were discontinued, Tom gave up hope of attending graduate school and began looking into the alternatives. In his reading about the war, he came to the conclusion that he could not serve in the military: "When I saw films showing the true brutality of the war, I just gradually decided that I could never bring myself to commit those things." He thought of becoming an officer and trying to stay out of Vietnam itself but decided "how terrible it would be for me to use my brains to make other men better killers." Finally, he decided to emigrate.

Tom's maternal grandparents emigrated from Czechoslovakia to the United States prior to World War I to escape conscription.

They are now deceased, but a great-aunt who immigrated with them is still living. This family background helped Tom's mother understand his move to Canada. His father's parents also emigrated from Czechoslovakia; his father, however, a World War II veteran, sees an obligation in military service and cannot accept the fact that his son has turned his back on his country. Tom is aware of his father's dilemma: "He's going to come and visit me and help me get established, but he will never be able to look at me in the same way that he will look upon some man who went off and served his country."

Indications of assimilation are difficult to observe in Tom's short time in K-W. Living in a university dormitory for the six weeks, he has been lonely without his fiancee and plagued with worries, probably unnecessarily, of something going wrong with her immigration to Canada. He seems to be waiting—waiting for Judy's arrival so they can get married, waiting for the school year to begin so they can both start graduate school; waiting, really, to become involved in the community. He finds himself referring to Canada as "your" country and America as "my" country. He gets defensive in the face of the extreme anti-American views of some Canadians. Tom is confident, though, that for him it will be only a matter of time before he is settled into K-W. Academically well-qualified, he sees opportunities similar to those in the United States.

Although in Canada, he has applied for a conscientious objector status under the new Supreme Court ruling which does not require formal religious grounds for such classification. Should he receive this status, he plans to serve alternate service in the States and then return permanently to Canada. In America, he says, "the system so completely wrecks the life of young people. The biggest thing that the war and the draft is doing is forcing young people to rearrange their lives. The human energy that is being lost— sooner or later this is going to manifest itself. The United States just cannot go on messing up its young people."

◆   ◆   ◆   ◆   ◆

There's quite a difference between St. Michael, Alaska and Kitchener-Waterloo, Ontario, but David and Jill's ideals did not change with their move. Once busy using their skills to better the lives of the poverty-stricken Eskimos in Alaska, they now find means of contributing to the middle- and working-class community of K-W.

"They won't let you stay and help your country. You try to help it, but you start getting the feeling it's not worth it. They're not listening to me anyway, so why not go and help better another country? Canada's here and they've got Indians to work with. We were employed by the government as Vista volunteers. Another government branch, Defense, outweighed it. It became quite clear what the priorities of the United States are."

After teaching for a year in a poverty section of a small Missouri town, David and Jill applied to Vista and were accepted in St. Michael, Alaska to work with Eskimos—forfeiting $12,000 they would have earned teaching, to work for a dollar a day. After helping to build a water tank and establishing a library in Alaska, David's draft board informed him that the only way to retain his draft exemption was by returning to teach in Missouri. "It was just the last straw." In September 1969, David and Jill headed for Canada, planning to work with Eskimos and Indians in their new country.

The decision to emigrate was easy to make. As a teenager, David had decided that "people really shouldn't kill and wars were sick." He grew increasingly disillusioned by the treatment of minority groups in the States. There were events such as the Democratic Convention of 1968. "I found myself being totally alienated by what was being done in the United States." His discontent grew until finally, with the notice from his draft board, "I no longer wanted any part of the U.S."

Another factor easing their decision was parental support. The family disapproval which causes anguish for many deserters and resisters was not an issue for them. David's parents raised him to make his own decisions and to be responsible for his own actions; they therefore respected his decision to move to Canada. Jill's parents were very much in favor of the move and gave them their final boost. They have expressed the wish that their other son-in-law who is fighting in Vietnam was also in Canada.

After a year in Canada, David and Jill are quite happy with the move. They will have to become citizens before they can do government work with Indians; in the meantime both have accepted teaching jobs at a local Mennonite school. Through the Mennonite church in which they are active they have made a number of friends. They feel life in Canada is better—the people more friendly and open-minded, with less polarization between those of opposing views; "they may disagree with you, but they'll respect your opinion."

David is studying Canadian history at the university and hopes eventually to get involved in politics. He sees Canada at a crossroads: she can either accept the policies of the United States by aligning herself with America, accepting her presuppositions on international affairs and strong-arming other nations to accept her positions, or Canada can work for world peace through non-violent means.

David and Jill are not sorry that they cannot return to the U.S.; during the year before he received his induction notice they could have returned and chose not to. Jill feels that the U.S. should grant draft-age emigrants amnesty, less for the sake of the emigrants than for the country's own good: "Although a lot of them wouldn't want to go back to the United States anyhow, . . . [America's] lost a lot of well-educated, qualified people." David is angered by the reason he cannot return: "It's not that I want to go back, not that I ever would if I could—it's just that my country—or the country that raised me and educated me—decided that I'm a criminal. They call me a criminal, not because I won't help people, but because I think it is more important for me to work with Eskimos than to teach in Missouri."

◆　　　◆　　　◆　　　◆　　　◆

Jerry made a moral decision not to cooperate with the selective service system. He has an extensive religious background in the

Episcopal church and several priests were willing to testify on his behalf. Although he had a good chance of receiving conscientious objector status, he chose not to accept this alternative. Jerry refused to apply for C.O. classification "because other men with similar beliefs against war and killing, but not extensive religious backgrounds, or who are simply less articulate, would probably not get a C.O. I could not use such an inequitable system."

Some draft resisters who have taken this stand are serving sentences in prison. For Jerry, jail was never a consideration: "It makes you ineffective. You have a stand, and all of a sudden your voice is cut off." Instead, Jerry, his wife Susan and their two-month-old son came to Canada in the summer of 1970. Both having grown up outside of Detroit, just a few miles from Ontario, they were familiar with Canada.

Their assimilation into Canadian life seems imminent. Jerry, a cellist, will be teaching music in the school system and privately. They are both relaxed and hopeful for their new life in Ontario. Canada seems much freer to them, and they feel that it is important to work on being good Canadians. While they express their opinions about the U.S. honestly, Jerry thinks that Canada is not the place for them to demonstrate against America.

Susan feels that they will make good Canadian citizens: "At a time when there's a lot of apathy going around, we were concerned enough to follow our consciences to refuse to participate in the war and made the major decision to come to Canada. We will take an interest in Canada, and try to keep it from becoming what we were against in the United States."

chapter 4
FATHERS AND THE FATHERLAND

The sincere dissenter is frequently expected to be capable of producing an articulate, rational argument of his beliefs. The Selective Service System in particular assumes that if such beliefs are genuine they must be derived from a system of belief which is the guiding force in the life of the dissenter.

Today there are many men who are not articulate, do not present a rationally developed argument, and hold no system of belief who nevertheless refuse to participate in the war in Southeast Asia and in the military system executing that war. Many young people reject "rational" approaches to problem solving, do not consider the ability to articulate especially virtuous, and find no system of belief useful for living in today's world. (For a further discussion, see "The Larger Picture.")

Other men have not had extensive education and training to develop the skills necessary to articulate their beliefs. Their refusal to be in the military is nevertheless based on their values and perceptions of the world. Jim, Skip, and Larry, all deserters from the U.S. military, are three such men.

Larry, the second child among eleven, experienced a tightly run regime at home, a life based on rules enforced by fear of punishment. During his school years his family moved 35 times; in high school Larry was forced into a college preparatory course by his father. Finding academic achievement very difficult, he dropped out of school in the tenth grade.

After Larry had left school, his father placed a 10 P.M. curfew on him. In his own car, but registered in his father's name, he was picked up at 11 P.M. for operating a "stolen vehicle"—on a complaint by his father. Soon after, Larry was ordered out of the house after an argument with his parents and was picked up at a friend's house two hours later as a runaway. For this offense, Larry had the bitter experience of spending Christmas in a juvenile home.

When he was released on New Year's Eve, he got drunk at a party, broke some furniture, resisted arrest, and was put in jail. A month later at his trial, Larry's father suggested to the judge that Larry be allowed to join the Army rather than do time on the juvenile farm. The judge agreed and on his seventeenth birthday, Larry enlisted.

During basic training his grandmother died and after being refused an emergency leave, he went A.W.O.L. Consequently he lost two months' pay and was confined to camp for the duration of basic training. A month later his sister eloped. He left without permission to visit her. His mother called the police who told the nearby air base's military police where he was. Larry was sentenced to 30 days in the stockade.

Larry mingled with Vietnam veterans during the next year. He heard stories of the killing of women and children, torture treatment of suspected Viet Cong, bombings of villages and what he considered an insane delight with napalm. He began to question his imminent participation in such events, finally deciding that he could not possibly fight a group of men labeled "the enemy" just because some officers had designated them as such.

Larry refused to obey orders which seemed senseless and arbitrary. He thought his father had issued nonsensical orders just to prove his own power to himself, and it seemed to Larry that the military acted in the same way. He asked for a pass to go to a nearby city to attend a meeting of his religion, scientology. The request was refused. This seemed unfair to Larry since passes were granted to men for less worthwhile activities. So again he went A.W.O.L. Three months later he attended a Vietnam moratorium demonstration without signing out, was followed, picked up and returned to the base for court-martial. Two days later he received his orders for Vietnam.

The next day Larry deserted. When he arrived at his home to pick up some savings bonds, his mother once again called the nearby air force base and arranged for her son's arrest. Larry was arrested, but in being transferred to his base, made a break for California and eventually Canada.

Larry experienced a great deal of pain while living with his family. He felt deserted by his parents as his father would make arbitrary commands and his mother and father would call the police to punish him. He thought that his parents' actions were not only cruel to him, but were wrong.

Likewise Larry was hurt by nonsensical and capricious orders from officers in the military. He felt it was right to go to your grandmother's funeral, it was right to talk to your sister when she eloped, it was right to practice your religion and it was wrong for the military to prevent you from doing these things, especially when other soldiers were granted similar privileges.

Unlike many draft resisters who are not faced with the draft until their college years, and who are able to take months or years to think through their stand on the whole issue of the military and the Vietnam war, Larry, at age 17, was suddenly given the choice of a juvenile farm or the Army. He used to obey orders in the Army which seemed senselessly to curb his freedom.

His dislike of the military was compounded by his increasing disapproval of the Vietnam war. Larry did not have the maturity to express articulately his opposition to the military—and perhaps did not see the necessity for such a process—but in the only way he knew, reached his decision not to participate in the killing.

◆　　　◆　　　◆　　　◆　　　◆

Skip, like Larry, had an unhappy childhood. His father was an alcoholic, and his mother did not want to spend much time with her children. For seven years, he lived with a great-aunt in another city. There he attended a boys' trade school, doing well in electronics and radio. When he moved back with his parents, he attended a regular high school.

Skip and his father got into a fight, and Skip had a charge of attempted manslaughter pressed on him by his father. As had happened to Larry, the judge gave Skip a choice between jail or joining the military. He chose the latter, although on his enlistment papers he noted opposition to all war and fighting and after basic training applied for a conscientious objector discharge.

Application for such a discharge requires interviews with a chaplain, a psychiatrist, and an officer "knowledgeable in policies and procedures relating to conscientious objector matters" (Department of Defense directive). The psychiatrist is to determine whether the applicant has any mental disorder which would warrant his separation from the military; usually the examination takes only a few minutes and the psychiatrist's report reads, "Free from any mental disease or disorder which would warrant disposition through medical channels." The report from the chaplain's interview with the applicant includes his conclusions about the sincerity of the man and an opinion as to the source of his belief. The officer who has the hearing is also required to prepare a statement including his recommendation and his reasons for it.

Skip had the three interviews. Even though he was relatively inarticulate, he had the impression that the chaplain thought him sincere. However, his application was denied.

Skip had been assigned to radio school. Soon after he received notice of his rejection for a C.O. discharge, he received orders to train officers in radio and electronic techniques. In one class, a lieutenant told him that he was "doing it all wrong." A verbal argument led to a physical one, Skip hitting his superior officer. Within three months he received orders for Vietnam. The next day he deserted.

He worked in Oregon under an assumed name for one month. During that time, he attempted to enter Canada but because he did not have enough money he was refused. (Visitors are normally required to have $10 for each day they intend to remain.) Eventually, though, Skip was admitted as a visitor. Struck by the beauty of British Columbia, he headed back to Vancouver despite job offers in three other areas of the country. He held a job there for three months until an economy cutback laid him off. The sparse savings on which he now lives have been further depleted by the purchase of a $550 engagement ring for his Canadian girl friend.

Skip, like Larry, suffered during his childhood. He too experienced the deep hurt of having his father press criminal charges against him and force him into the military.

♦   ♦   ♦   ♦   ♦

Jim was the oldest of eight children. His father had been a heavy drinker for years, especially since the family went on welfare when Jim was about ten. One of his earliest memories is that of being hit by a cup thrown by his father in a drunken tantrum.

Through elementary and junior high school, Jim's grades were good; upon entering high school he requested a college prep course. A guidance counselor felt this would be foolish, however, since his family did not have money to send him through college and would not enroll Jim in the course. Consequently, Jim found school boring and of little value. When his family had a desperate need for more money during his sophomore year he dropped out and went to work.

After working for three months, Jim became angry that most of his income was used to keep the family alive, while all other money paid for his father's alcohol. "So I quit my job and played his game for a year, and just sat flat on my can and didn't even attempt to find work." During this period his mother worked, so while at home Jim was "literally raising two of the children." In retrospect Jim showed considerable understanding of his father, but at 16 he felt only anger and hostility.

While at home, Jim continued studying on his own. "Even when I quit school I knew the need for education. I've always liked history and social sciences. Classical literature was one of my favorites—I read quite extensively in ancient Greek and Roman authors." He was also building a small library from the Harvard University classics.

At 18, Jim, who was expecting to be drafted anyway, enlisted to get away from the unhappy home. He had always wanted to go to Europe, so he requested assignment in Germany. His request was accepted and he went to Munich in early 1966. While there, he enjoyed his work as an X-ray technician and in many ways was a model soldier. "I read the *Stars and Stripes* (an Army newspaper) faithfully. I didn't oppose the war; in fact I favored it, the way it was presented to me—that the South Vietnamese were earnestly trying to prevent the Communists from conquering and ruling them and that the United States was sincerely trying to help these people. The news we got was that our people were doing a great job."

While in Germany Jim received word of more trouble at home. He finally went back to have his father committed to a hospital for his alcoholism. The next year he volunteered for duty in Vietnam, arriving in July 1967. Vietnam, however, was not as he had imagined it. "Something was wrong. Everything was just about at the opposite pole of what I had read. Most of the people, contrary to news reports, not only did not have their heart in the war, but they wanted no part of that stinking mess. What the Vietnamese need is food, and a better standard of living, and we were steadily taking this away from them through the war."

Jim worked in a hospital, often with civilians, as an X-ray technician, and in that position he grew more and more frustrated. He became keenly aware of the extensive human suffering.

The manner in which many GI's treated Vietnamese added to Jim's disillusionment. "Quite a few GI's disliked the Vietnamese. They were lower than life. This was brought out in what they called them—gooks and slopes—and their treatment of them, even in the hospitals."

He became angry with the military for having duped him into believing that the war was "right," and equally angry with himself for having volunteered to fight in Vietnam. Lacking means to express these anti-war feelings, he kept them to himself.

After his term of duty finished, Jim returned home. The feeling that he ought to do something to help persisted; he finally concluded that it was the mass media whose excellent presentation of the war as both necessary and successful played a key role in the continuation of the war. Along the same lines, though, Jim felt that if he "could devise a way to get the facts about the war in Vietnam to the American public, then there would be public pressure on the government to stop it now." He decided to establish a news service coming out of Vietnam which would give the American people "the facts about what was really happening."

In March 1969, he requested another tour of Vietnam duty to set up the service and begin to collect information. Instead, he was assigned to Thailand. When he arrived, he immediately asked for an intra-theater transfer to Vietnam. While waiting to be transferred, he made an unsuccessful attempt to cross the Laotian border and he instead probed into the revolutionary activity in Thailand's northern provinces.

His request of transfer was granted, and Jim was given a month's leave in the States. While home he began making contacts for the storage and publication of material which would be produced by his Vietnam news service. In Canada he went to the Aid Centers to seek advice. Most people told him that the American public had heard the truth, that many had been speaking out against the war for five years and more, and yet people still refused to listen or to believe.

Jim went back home, confused and discouraged. "I thought the information I had would compel belief. But that's not what everybody was telling me. It seemed hopeless." He found himself caught: he had no desire to go back to Vietnam if he could not work on his news service, and unless his time in the military could be spent constructively, helping end the war, he wanted no part of it at all. Jim's eventual conclusion, reached in 72 hours without sleep, was that he could not do either without being punished; "I just didn't want to spend any time in the stockade. That seemed like such a waste." After the agony of those three days, Jim gave up his news service and left for Canada. He is a man who will try to work for change in the United States but who has found that he must do it north of the border.

Jim, Skip, and Larry had difficult family situations with which to cope as young children. Their histories are not pleasant or ideal. For this, they may be condemned by many and cited as examples of "the kind of men we're glad to have leave the country."

There are those who would not consider their acts conscientious. Their decisions were not arrived at through intellectual experience or exercise. Yet they are men who were unable to tolerate or participate in the Vietnam war. They developed a visceral response compelling them to say "no" to agony and destruction.

chapter 5
THE EAGLE
SCOUT

"My father used to walk around in his West Point robe on weekends. I never understood why that experience was so important to him. We had a close relationship except when it came to West Point—he was really reluctant to talk about it. He would just wear that robe. It was really sad."

Daniel Mulby's father, whose family had lived in America since the 1620's, was accused of cheating on a French exam during his third year at West Point. He could have left the Point immediately and not faced a court-martial. But he knew he was innocent and thought that his innocence would be proved at the court-martial. Instead he was found guilty, expelled from West Point and given a dishonorable discharge. Such a discharge stands in the way of obtaining many jobs since it is often considered equal to a felony conviction.

Dan's father worked in the Philadelphia navy yard during the war, his dishonorable discharge not an obstacle under those conditions. He attended Temple University and the Drexel Institute of Technology in the evenings, eventually passing the Pennsylvania Professional Engineering exam. Yet he never liked his engineering job; in fact, he disliked most of the many jobs he had, and neither was he a success at them, earning only a little over

$7,000 a year when he died in 1965. His was a life full of frustration.

When he was 11, Dan, an only child, and his parents moved to upper New York State. At that time, he joined a boy scout troop. Scouting continued to be an important part of his life through high school. As an eagle scout he received the God and Country award through the Episcopal Church, was in the Order of the Arrow and was leader for the Order of the Arrow in his region. Church activities were also important; Dan was an acolyte throughout high school.

Dan's high school was small, with 33 in his graduating class in 1963. He won eleven letters in track, football and basketball, had a grade average of 91 and ranked fifth in his class. He spent his first year in college at the University of Toledo. Along with some friends, he transferred to the University of Wisconsin at Madison the next year.

At Toledo he did some thinking about the draft and the military. He felt an obligation to do something for his country and, knowing that he would be drafted, decided that his years in the armed forces should be as productive as possible and therefore he decided he should be an officer. He signed up for Reserved Officer Training Corps—a four year course which would grant him a commission in the Army as a second lieutenant.

In joining ROTC Dan also thought he would be doing something for his father. He would get the commission that his father had not gotten and had wanted so badly. Dan never talked to his father about it, but he knew it would please him.

Once in ROTC, Dan's ideas underwent changes. When he first joined, he felt that "it didn't bother me at all. It was just like boy scouts!" In the summer of 1966, between his sophomore and junior years at Wisconsin, he went to Ft. Reilly, Kansas, for six weeks of military training. He was disturbed by the attitude of drill sergeants and others, who called the Vietnamese gooks and slopeheads. Equally disturbing was the nature of the infantry training. During bayonet practice, the soldiers were required to shout,

"Kill, Kill, Kill," as they charged the "enemy." "It finally hit me that I was being trained to kill. It hadn't hit me before! ROTC was no longer like the boy scouts."

Over the same time period, Dan's ideas about the war in Southeast Asia were also changing. During his first year at Wisconsin he supported increased involvement of the U.S. military. Goldwater ran for president that year, and the arguments on the war and other issues were constant and intense in the dormitory where he lived. Increasingly, however, Dan doubted the validity of his own positions. In the spring of 1967, a demonstration was held at the university to protest the presence of recruiters from Dow Chemical Company, then the chief supplier of napalm for use by the U.S. forces in Vietnam. When Dan expressed to a friend his feeling that the demonstrators were probably right, he was asked why he did not join them. Dan's reluctance stemmed from the difficulties he might encounter with ROTC and from a personal uneasiness with demonstrating as a form of expression for himself. Overwhelming in impact, however, was the counter-demonstration in which four respected members of Dan's ROTC class participated. Noticing the signs they carried—such as one reading "Napalm is good for V.C. acne"—Dan felt repelled by the inhumanity of which he, as a fellow army officer, would be a part.

One of the last papers that he was assigned to write for ROTC before receiving his commission was an intelligence report on North Vietnam. Using his skills as a history major, Dan carefully studied the history of Vietnam with an emphasis on the period prior to 1954—the year the Geneva accords were signed ending the French-Indochina war. He concluded that the United States was fighting historical forces which were impossible to control by military activity, being deeply rooted in the society and culture of Vietnam. Eventually Dan decided that not only was military defeat of these forces impossible but that even to fight them was immoral and an unjustifiable intervention in the affairs of the Vietnamese people.

Dan reached this decision three months before he was to receive his commission from ROTC. To be a military officer, almost certainly in Vietnam, had become contrary to his belief about U.S. action in that country. Yet refusal of his commission would mean that he would be drafted; not only would he be unable to complete his undergraduate work but he would still be in a position contradictory to his moral understandings of the U.S. military in Vietnam.

To solve the dilemma, he decided to utilize his history of medical problems. During the spring of 1967 he tried to get a physical discharge from ROTC and the military so he would neither be commissioned nor drafted. However, the military considered him healthy enough to be an officer. In June 1967 Dan was commissioned as a Second Lieutenant in the Transportation Corps of the 5th Army; later he was transferred to the military police.

Because Dan had one more year to complete his undergraduate work, he was permitted to serve in the Reserves. He expected to be called to active duty once he received his degree, but when he was accepted into a program leading to a master's degree in education and certification for teaching American history on the secondary school level, the Army allowed him to continue in the reserves.

During the summer of 1968 Dan worked as a ranger in a New York state park near his home. He watched the demonstration at the Democratic convention in Chicago and the Russian invasion of Czechoslovakia on television. "It was hard to see the difference in the two events," Dan said. "Repression of dissent in Chicago is like repression of dissent in Prague."

That fall he began his graduate program. Constantly aware of the choice he would have to make when he faced active duty in two years, he went to see a campus minister at the university to talk about his situation and the anxiety it caused. Although the minister could not present any options Dan had not thought of, he was sympathetic and helped him build up his confidence to face the situation. Dan visited him often during the next two years.

During his first semester at graduate school Dan met informally with other persons in the degree program to talk about the ineffectiveness and the dehumanizing aspects of American education. They decided that one way they could work for change while they were still students was to organize a group in the College of Education to work for curriculum reform and change in the methods and techniques of teacher-training. The Education Student Association was formed.

Dan published the E.S.A.'s newsletter and was an active proponent of free schools. He was instrumental in the organization of three free schools, where children learn in an unrestricted environment conducive to creativity and experimentation. Dan's activity with the E.S.A. was respected within the College of Education, even by those who did not necessarily agree with his philosophy of education. He and the E.S.A. were given permission to address faculty meetings of the college, and Dan was given a research assistantship.

Within the bounds presented by being a reserve army officer, he did what he could to protest the war. He wrote a number of articles and letters to the E.S.A. newsletter on the immorality of the war, and wrote to the student newspaper protesting the existence of ROTC on the Wisconsin campus, signing it "a dissident officer." During the fall of 1969, Dan did his practice teaching in Racine, Wisconsin, where he became very active in the anti-war movement writing and publishing leaflets.

Active duty was still very much on his mind. The options as he saw them were going to jail or going into the army to organize in the growing G.I. dissent movement. He could do that, he thought, since he had done well organizing in the E.S.A. and in the anti-war movement in Racine. The idea of being in the military carrying out the war that he abhorred was, however, repugnant to him.

Dan did not consider a conscientious objector discharge as an option. He knew that very few such discharges are given, and it would be unlikely that the Army, having trained him for four years and paid him a salary for two, would be willing to discharge him. His primary reason for not applying for a C.O. discharge, however, was that he was not a pacifist. He did not claim that he would not fight in all wars, or that all violence was wrong, but he felt no less strongly that the war in Vietnam was very wrong and that he would have nothing to do with it.

At that time he had also ruled out emigration to Canada as an alternative. As a boy he had lived near the Canadian border. In his small town, prejudice against Canadians was prevalent, and Dan had disliked a number of the Canadians whom he had known personally. That particular prejudice was still a factor in his life.

Toward the end of the first semester in his last school year, Dan again attempted to obtain a physical discharge from the Army. He went through a number of physical examinations, made especially grueling by several officers who realized that he was trying to get out of the service. He got a letter from a psychiatrist saying that he was unfit for active duty. Still, the decision came down that he was fit and that he would be called for active duty after his June graduation. He continued to work for a discharge: a letter from an Army psychiatrist said he should be transferred from the military police to a desk job; a Navy doctor recommended that he not be called because of a skin disease which Dan had had for a long time. He wrote a number of letters to his congressman, who finally appealed the decision to the Surgeon General of the United States. The Surgeon General affirmed Dan's mental and physical fitness.

Regardless of official decisions, Dan knew that he could not serve in the Army. His feelings against the war were so strong that he could not even look at himself in the mirror in uniform. By February 1970, Dan's opposition to military service had overridden his prejudice against Canadians, and he made plans to go to Toronto in June with a friend whose beliefs and experience with the military had been similar. The two men talked of establishing a center in Toronto where newly arrived American immigrants could come and in a relaxing, friendly atmosphere work through the meaning of their act and decide what their next steps would be. They thought that films and other art forms could be experimented with at the center to help new arrivals with this process.

The men arrived in Toronto on June 25th and soon discovered that a deserter-resister organization, Red, White and Black, was with some other groups developing the kind of center they envisioned—The Hall. Dan has worked full time in that development since he arrived in Canada; he has made no other long-range plans.

Many men in Canada have undergone a process of changing convictions, as Dan did. Draft resisters especially have frequently had four years of college during which their awareness and understanding developed; although "all-American boys" in high school and the first year or two of college, they later conclude that the U.S. military involvement in Vietnam is wrong and that much of American society is rigid, closed to experimentation with new values and life styles.

Dan has not faced a question which eventually confronts most of the emigrants: "How can I work for political change in the United States when I am in Canada?" This dilemma has plagued an increasing number of men, especially since the Pan-Canadian Conference of May 1970, where several speakers emphasized the need to return to the U.S. to bring about change there by living and working underground.

A few have returned to America to organize for change; this is a very small minority, however. A larger number have taken the position that the emigration of 30,000 men from the United States has political value; this movement, they say, is forcing more and more Americans to look at their government's policies in Vietnam.

The majority of the deserters and resisters in Canada resolve this question by saying that they are no longer concerned about changing the United States. Many think it hopeless for them—or anyone—to actually change the U.S. government. Having chosen to live in Canada, participation in politics—should they choose to become involved—would be in Canadian politics.

chapter 6
THE PIONEER

John Ernst's family came to an immigrant town in southeastern Minnesota from Bavaria four generations ago. The land along the southern border of the state is some of the most fertile in the Midwest, so the community flourished. A meat packing plant went up, and John's father, a trained butcher, went to work there as a hamboner.

John and his brother were raised strictly according to the work ethic which had been an integral part of that community since its inception: there is a time for work and a time for play—but the time for play comes only after all work is done. Hard work was understood as the way to achieve all that is worthwhile, revered not just for itself but because only through work could man maintain independence, his most important possession.

Through most of high school John, captain of his school's football team, was involved in church activities. His immigrant ancestors four generations back had been Lutherans, his grandfather was a Lutheran minister, and he was a member of the largest Lutheran church in town. He could remember when their church services had been held in German. During the 1960 Presidential campaign, however, John had a confrontation with his minister whose anti-Kennedy stand he felt was based on religious prejudice. He also interpreted the minister's active political stance as an attempt to dictate his own decision about the candidates. Then in college, John concluded that the Lutheran church was an advocate of political status quo in America as it had been in Nazi Germany despite its ostensible endorsement of church-state separation. John felt that his independence was threatened by the church, and so except during vacations at home he never again attended the services.

John's political thinking reflected two influences. At the University of Minnesota, he became convinced that the war in Vietnam was wrong—a conflict in which he could not participate. Although he took part in some anti-war demonstrations and was personally close to one professor who opposed the war, John neither considered himself a political activist nor saw much value in such activity. A family friend who had been a farm-laborite in the 1930's, a defender of religious objection to World War II, and an opponent of McCarthyism in the early 1950's, had at age 65 a long string of defeats behind him, a few mild successes, and an enlightened cynicism about the possibilities for change in the United States. To John, this man had fought all his life for nothing, and through him he had come to the conclusion that political activism was essentially meaningless. John saw in the friend what he might become himself if he were to take up causes in the U.S.

Near the end of John's freshman year at the university, his father developed agonizing terminal cancer. After several months of the extreme grief and anxiety of caring for her dying husband, Mrs. Ernst committed suicide. John dropped out of school to make his mother's funeral arrangements and then nursed his father for four months until his death in 1964. Again, he bore the burden of the funeral arrangements since his brother was in Formosa studying at the time.

Struck by oppressive grief, John needed to get away from everybody and everything he knew. Camping his way west, he met, while in the Rockies, a couple from British Columbia. From their descriptions of their home province, John decided that he wanted to visit it. The Canadians told him that if he was interested in going to B.C. before they returned, they had friends who would certainly let him stay at their home. Intrigued, John headed for the province, found the family who had been recommended, and stayed for two weeks. He enjoyed his visit and decided that sometime in the future he would return to live.

Meanwhile, John returned to Minnesota and finished his undergraduate work in history. For graduate work, he was accepted into programs in medieval studies at the University of Toronto and the University of Michigan and chose the Canadian school. Although in 1967 draft boards were still granting deferments to graduate students and thus John had no immediate problems with the military, he had decided that he would not submit to induction in any case during the war in Vietnam. John looked at the draft as an institution rather like the church: archaic, dehumanizing, bound with inane customs and rituals. John's assertation of his independence led him to ignore the local board and the selective service system by refusing to be inducted and refusing to struggle for a deferment: "One of the draft rituals is a game played by many middle-class men called 'getting a deferment or exemption or finding any other way out of the draft.' I refuse to grovel! I have never tried to buy time and I will not start now. I could try numerous dodges, but I will not lower myself to that. Groveling would reduce my humanity and the humanity of the members of the local draft board. Groveling puts the registrant's life in hands that have no moral right to control it and presumes that the draft board's power is legitimate."

Even though he had done well during his first year of graduate work, John concluded that the academic life of a scholar-teacher was not what he wanted. During the summer of 1968 he asked Susan, an American art student in Toronto, to marry him and go with him to Vancouver to realize his earlier dream of living in British Columbia.

John did not feel forced to go to Canada; instead, he considered it his choice to live outside the "intrusions of the American authoritarian society." In a letter to Susan, at home in Rochester before their wedding, he wrote:

"I have a choice of leaving the country or remaining and fighting for years for a deferment. The U.S. has no compelling attraction for me and fighting for deferments appeals to me less. Canada is a beautiful land. It is a very easy choice.

"The Southeast Asian War is only one part of the America we are leaving. It is an exemplary part though, showing how innocuous little scratches turn into huge cancerous wounds. The U.S. is the bully on the block, the world bandit painted as the policeman and world sheriff for American allies to believe and trust in. From a small-town, manifest destiny mentality one can expect little more of the majority of the American people. The propaganda network is so neatly worked into people's jobs that to criticize is to resign from the American economy. I cannot blame plastic America and napalm America on all Americans who voted for Johnson or who will vote for Nixon. That doesn't do any good.

"I can only opt out of it and try to create a life as independently as I can. The draft is only one of my gripes with the U.S.; it is an arm of the cancer which was about to drag me down with it. The cancer we can escape, not by living in Toronto, which suffers under some of the same madness as any big city in the U.S, but by homesteading and buying land where we can create our own environment and be relatively free of the authorities that seek to control lives through pocketbooks. This is not a bitter choice, motivated mostly by repulsion from the U.S, but a combination of two forces: antipathy for the U.S. way of life, the Organization Man, the Public Man, and attraction for the land on Vancouver Island with its openness and seclusion."

In British Columbia, John enrolled in a university course which granted him a teacher's certificate. While there, he and Susan became good friends with Peter, a draft resister, and his wife Jane. Peter introduced the Ernsts to Larry, also a draft resister, and Linda, his wife, whom he had met at the University of Wisconsin.

All three couples shared John's dream of owning and working their own land, as free of confining and dehumanizing institutions as possible. One Saturday, really on a lark, the three women contacted a realtor on Vancouver Island who showed them a

150-acre farm for $50,000. They fell in love with it instantly and called their husbands, who shared their enthusiasm. Peter negotiated a loan with an uncle, and the land was theirs.

The land included pastures, trees, and gardens, a two bedroom house, garage and a car-port. The Group W Bench Partnership, as they called themselves, had a beautiful home on a magnificent island: Vancouver Island, a lush green surrounded by the grey of tall mountains and the unpolluted blue of Puget Sound.

The first summer, 1969, contained hard work, few results, and many guests. Friends and relatives who heard the story of the paradise came to see. But because of the seriousness of their venture, the group had developed a possessiveness toward their land which made numerous guests unwelcome; visitors were called Bench-warmers. People who happened onto the farm from the hippie community expecting open fires and a warm welcome were met with quiet nonacceptance. Several hip people have tried to crash on the 150 acres, one group with a circus, only to be turned away.

From the beginning, the group has never seem themselves as a commune in the usual sense. They are not conducting a social experiment with extended families or shared incomes or encounter techniques. Group W was formed because three couples wanted to own and farm their own land, and no one couple could afford a farm of their own. They are good friends who trust each other enough to assume the mortgage on a $50,000 farm.

The six function more as couples than they do as a group. It is from spouses that help and advice is asked, whether others are around or not. About five meals each week are eaten communally, the others prepared and eaten by couples alone. Rebecca was born to Jane and Peter in June 1970. The birth strengthened the community by bringing the couples closer together. All six help with feeding, diaper changing, and care of the child. Because of the extremely busy life that each person leads, the group decided that it was imperative to the health of the community to set aside one evening each week to discuss the farm, their life in the group, and their future.

The group has cleared seven acres, planted vegetables in four of them, and is raising hens, a goat, a few calves, and bees. Neighbor farmers freely give advice to them, and books on horticulture and animal husbandry fill their bookshelves. Larry and Lynn have enclosed the garage for their use as a house. Peter and Jane have taken over the building of their home from a local carpenter, who put up the frame. During the 1969-70 school year, John and Peter taught high school, while Larry taught at a local college. All of the wives were students. Since the men found that teaching took too much time from the farm, John and Peter quit their jobs after one year, and Larry only taught part-time during the 1970-71 school year. If additional money was needed, John and Peter plan to take logging jobs which would take less time than teaching.

As the group plans its future with discussions of ten- and fifteen-year plans, the question of their relationship with the "outside" world is often discussed. Jane, the youngest member, feels that it would be selfish for the group to spend their lives totally on their land, hoarding the 150 acres for their own use. The other five have considered working the land to be the initial priority. The three men found that for them it had become futile to try to change America; they had come to Canada to be free for themselves. The group tries to remain open to Jane's position and encourage her not to get frustrated by their seeming insensitivity. There has been talk of helping other draft resisters once the farm does not require their total energies.

John is under indictment in the States for not appearing for his induction. He will never be able to go home again. Yet he does not care. He has created a new home with his own hands in the same pioneer spirit possessed by his relatives who came to Minnesota 100 years ago.

chapter 7
THE CLINIC

Stewart Alsop described it in *Newsweek* as "a profoundly depressing place," but to young people and those servicing the youth culture the Toronto Free Youth Clinic is a place of significance and hope. It offers to youth medical treatment and advice; drug users in particular find help given with understanding and without judgment. It seems almost like an act of reparations for young people who have dropped out of the conventional society they do not accept—and which many feel never accepted them.

The remarkable nature of the clinic is underscored by the American staff, including two deserters. J.C. is a twenty-one-year-old white from Florida; Sam, a black man from suburban Washington, D.C., is twenty. Although there are some similarities, their stories contrast vividly.

J.C. had led a relatively uneventful life until his mother died when he was a teenager. After her death, his father began to move around the state, going from job to job, and their family life gradually fell apart. By the time he was seventeen, J.C. had left home, and before graduating from high school, he dropped out.

A greatly admired older brother had enlisted in the Marines, and on his eighteenth birthday, J.C. enlisted too. He first tried the Marines, but they had a waiting list. "I went next door to the

Coast Guard. 'This is great. I can get stationed in my home town and travel in those pretty white boats and run down rum runners and smugglers.' But they had a larger waiting list than the Marines. So did the Navy and so did the Air Force. So I went to the Army and they said, 'Sure, kid,' and so I enlisted. I didn't even know how long I had enlisted for, so I asked this man in uniform and he laughed and said twenty years. I didn't know what to do!"

While in basic training, chinks began to develop in the "traditional American ideas" which he had never questioned before. He qualified for Officer's Candidate School but joined the medical corps instead because he had decided that it was a more useful form of service, "the only humane thing the Army offered." When his older brother was reported killed in Vietnam (while in fact he had been seriously wounded), J.C. began questioning further the Army and the war. Most formative for him was the year he was stationed in San Antonio. He spent time talking with people in the anti-war coffee houses and began to work on projects in the San Antonio ghetto.

J.C. decided that he had to get out of the military and would first use the channels within the system. He applied for a conscientious objector discharge and was put in a holding platoon— "That's a place where they put people waiting special discharges, mental discharges, homosexual discharges, and so on. A lot of beautiful people . . . some of whom were waiting the same action I was. This time strengthened my opinions and beliefs."

While waiting for the decision, J.C. found himself arrested for smoking marijuana. After a month in jail the charges were dropped, but he missed a bed-check and was put in pre-trial confinement. In the prison he was falsely classified as a homosexual, placed in solitary confinement for twenty-seven days, and then sent to the stockade for six months.

While in prison he complained one evening when the lights were turned off while he was writing in his diary, and he was badly beaten. He was refused permission to see a doctor and only after several requests over a six-day period did J.C. get to see the commanding officer—who did not believe his story. An Army psychiatrist finally examined him, took him seriously, and an investigation was begun which led to the guard's court-martial. J.C. felt, though, that ". . . people in the high echelons . . . did of course remain unscathed."

His applications and appeals for C.O. discharge had been repeatedly rejected. Fearing that he would be sent to Vietnam, J.C. gave up his attempt to work through the system. He decided to desert. His unit sergeant gave him $10 and wished him well, and a friend forged a discharge on official forms. After a close brush with his commanding officer who had heard a rumor that he was deserting, J.C. headed for Canada, arriving in Toronto on January 31, 1969.

J.C. believes his was a rational decision. "I'm leaving that situation behind, not just to leave it, not to leave it without aiding in any way, but to leave it constructively. I can keep doing what I am doing now at the clinic and try my damnedest to prevent the situation in Canada from being too much infected by the situation in the U.S."

Sam, a 20-year-old black deserter, grew up in a middle class suburb in Virginia. His parents worked for the Federal government, and after high school he entered college. Sam feels that as a boy he had little contact with racism personally; as a young man he was outside of the black power movement.

When a close friend was killed in Vietnam, Sam decided to enlist: to see for himself what the war was like and to avenge, if possible, the death of his friend. He joined the Seabees and was stationed at Gulfport, Mississippi, and then went to Vietnam.

There he began to work in a clinic for the Vietnamese people in his spare time, making the discovery that helping human beings, both peasants and Viet Cong, was of great importance to him. Eventually he transferred from the Seabees into a Navy medical unit. During his tour in Vietnam, Sam increasingly questioned the U.S. government's policies. "I saw it as a great game, almost like a Monopoly game that is so complex you were tired of it. The only difference was that you were killing people and a nation's 'pride' was at stake."

After a year in Vietnam, Sam returned to the States, landing in Birmingham, Alabama. Although he had not noticed racism as a child, it struck him forcefully: "My first thought was how great it was to be back home, and then I began to notice the hate stares. After all I had been through, I had returned to racist America, and I was keenly aware of it."

Upon returning to his base after his leave, Sam began to consider emigrating to Canada. Two friends talked him out of it until his second tour in Vietnam loomed before him. At that point, he made up his mind to leave. "I get into things to learn and that's why I went to Vietnam." But he had concluded that the fighting was futile, a tragic waste of human life and resources. Furthermore, the United States "had cheated itself. It's ugly now." He decided that he could no longer be a part of the U.S. because of its war and racist society. "I just couldn't serve the U.S. in any way and didn't want to play their game or use their rules in any way."

Sam and a friend simply loaded up their car and drove from Gulfport to Washington. Sam's parents "thought I was homesick and had gone AWOL. When I stayed around for over a month, they knew I was serious, and in trouble." He then caught a plane to Toronto and has not been back to the States since.

In Canada, Sam experienced little emotional trauma or racial prejudice. Moving into the youth subculture, "the biggest culture shock I've had is calling an icebox a 'fridge'." Both his interests and medical skills are utilized in his work at the clinic. Starting as a volunteer, Sam is now on the staff, working over 60 hours a week for subsistence wages. Happy with what he is doing, he feels that he is contributing to genuine needs and concerns. Although he regrets not being able to visit his family, particularly his grandmother, he says he would not go back to the States— "unless it regresses 500 years, with no cities, no people, and no racism!"

Both J.C. and Sam have left their country with all that they see it standing for, and they have effectively entered Canadian life by serving others. Their work is long and demanding, unglamorous, with little material reward as incentive. But both are finding fulfillment—for them, what life is all about.

chapter 8
THE LARGER PICTURE

THE EXODUS AND CANADIAN
INDEPENDENCE

"In my opinion the most unpopular war that this country has
ever waged, not even excepting the Vietnam conflict, was our
second war with Great Britain. . . . Thomas Jefferson said
that the conquest of Canada would only be a matter of march-
ing—but it turned out to be a matter of fighting as well,
since the British, instead of 'rising as one man' to 'throw off
the British yoke' . . . showed a perverse disposition to fight
for King and country."

Samuel Eliot Morison, *et al.*
Dissent in Three American Wars,
(Cambridge, Mass.: Harvard
University Press, 1970)

The United States and Canada share a common border of over
2,500 miles and thus have good reasons for wanting to stay
friends. Despite modern armaments and the obvious military su-
periority of the U.S., any serious disagreement or falling out
could present grave problems to both nations, but particularly to
the U.S., a super-power. Cuba, a much smaller and poorer country
than Canada, became more than a thorn in the U.S. flesh when it

began receiving Russian nuclear weapons. Imagine the threat a hostile Canada would be to the U.S. which already perceives vast threats to its national security. The difficulties that a belligerent China has created for the vastly better equipped and industrialized Soviet Union constitute a model for the direction relations between competitive neighboring nations may go. Still, to suggest that Canada and the U.S. could be anything but firm friends and partners seems preposterous. There is much that continually cements the good relations that now exist between the two countries.

Canada, more than any other developed nation, has received a steady and expanding proportion of U.S. economic resources; this has led in fact to American dominance of the Canadian economy. There are few major corporations in Canada not affected directly by this economic might.

By the end of the 1950's seventy percent of Canadian imports were from the U.S., seventy-five percent of foreign investments came from the south, over fifty percent of Canada's manufacturing industry was owned or controlled by the U.S., and an even larger percentage of natural resources. On the other side, sixty percent of Canada's exports went to the south. The opening of the St. Lawrence Seaway in 1959 by Queen Elizabeth and President Eisenhower symbolized dramatically the "economic integration" of North America. The 1960's saw the continual growth of U.S. economic involvement and Canadian dependence upon her giant neighbor.

In music and the arts, most aspects of the youth culture which developed in the U.S. have inundated Canada. Despite the existence of creative film makers, rock musicians and designers in Canada, the market in film, music and fashions has been controlled by Madison Avenue and Hollywood. This has even been the case with serious art: American theatre, painting and sculpture, ballet and music are often more popular among Canadians than is native art.

Official statements from the Canadian government reaffirm the friendly relationship that exists between the two countries. Prime

Minister Pierre Trudeau's visit to Washington in 1969, one of the first by a foreign Chief of State to President Nixon, was marked by cordiality; and in a foreign affairs white paper issued in June, 1970, the U.S. was characterized as Canada's "closest friend and ally."

Nevertheless, a growing Canadian nationalism has produced a reaction to U.S. economic and cultural dominance, reflected in a rise in anti-American sentiment. In addition, frequent insensitivity to Canadian national pride and independence on the part of U.S. officials has contributed to this increasing friction. On January 15, 1970, George Ball, former U.S. Undersecretary of State, told the Committee on External Affairs of the House of Commons that Canada should avoid neutrality in its foreign policy. In response to Trudeau's decision to reduce Canada's commitment to NATO by two-thirds by 1970, Ball stated: "Many in the U.S. feel that Canada must carry a part of the North American defense burden. Otherwise, we will feel that we have been had." In the same speech, he went on to discuss the use of North American resources. A multinational corporation, he indicated, should control these and would make the best use of Canada's natural resources. In a book Ball had written in the previous year, he predicted that Canada would join the U.S. because Canadians would not be content much longer to get inferior wages as the price of independence. He was asked about that prediction in the committee meeting and answered, "The result was so acerbic as to purge my mind of any lingering doubts as to the vitality of Canadian nationalism." (*New York Times,* Jan. 16, 1970.)

Mr. Ball's speech to the committee did not restore his popularity in Canada. All three of Toronto's daily newspapers included a critical response to his speech in their editorials. During that same week a subsidiary of Standard Oil of New Jersey struck oil near the mouth of the Mackensie River. Pierre Trudeau was asked in Commons if he could assure that any deal selling more oil to the U.S. would not include handing over of any degree of control of any of Canada's water resources to the U.S. or the lessening in any way of their country's sovereignty over their Arctic water.

Trudeau answered that he could give that assurance. (*New York Times*, Jan. 17, 1970.) In 1969 the supertanker *Manhattan* with the help of Canadian icebreakers made a voyage through the Northwest passage. Canadians were angry. In April, 1970 the *Manhattan* was about to make its second voyage. The U.S. Congress had also appropriated fifty-nine million dollars to build a fleet of Coast Guard icebreakers capable of supplanting the Canadian icebreakers that assisted the *Manhattan* on her first voyage. Now Canadians were horrified. (*New York Times*, April 5, 1970.)

On April 8 the Trudeau government introduced legislation to apply Canadian pollution regulations to shipping in Arctic waters within one hundred miles of Canadian soil. T. C. Douglas, leader of the New Democratic Party, an opposition party, supported it by saying, "We want to make it clear to our friends south of the border that we will not tolerate anyone pushing the Canadian Government around." (*New York Times*, April 9, 1970.) At the same time, legislation was introduced to increase Canada's sovereignty over the sea from three miles to twelve miles. Again control of Canada's water, land and mineral resources was the motivation. (*New York Times*, April 17, 1970.)

The next day the State Department sent a note to Ottawa rejecting the right of Canada to exercise such jurisdiction. Ottawa agreed with the State Department that there was no basis in international law for such legislation. Trudeau stated that "distinctly Canadian considerations were more important than international ones." He added, "Part of our heritage is our wilderness. We cannot wait for a disaster to prompt us to act. We need law now to protect coastal states from the excesses of shipping states. We now know that spring is not automatic. We now know that the responsibility is ours to restore and maintain the health of the biosphere." (*New York Times*, April 19, 1970.)

Trudeau distinguished the Canadian experience from that of the U.S. "The frontiers of Canada have been rugged and as challenging as those anywhere in the world, but in certain important respects they reflect distinctly Canadian characteristics. Violence was not commonplace in our West and is not part of our North. In Canada, the law preceded the cattleman and prospector." (*New York Times,* April 17, 1970.)

The *New York Times* said that no Canadian could fail to perceive that in his reference to "shipping states" or in his statement "Canadians are not inhibited or directed by pressure of manifest destiny," that the Prime Minister was talking about the U.S.

Commons voted to extend the three mile limit and the pollution control bill without a dissenting vote. (*New York Times,* April 26, 1970.) In response to U.S. opposition Trudeau did agree to go to international tribunals over Canada's claim to the twelve mile limit. However, he refused to go to a world court over the pollution law. "We will not go to Court until such time as the law catches up with technology." (*New York Times,* April 19, 1970.)

In March President Nixon ordered a reduction of the amount of oil purchased from Canada from 634,692 barrels per day to 395,000. In a letter sent by a White House staff person to Senators protesting the move, it was stated that the reductions would not end until a resource pact had been culminated by Canada and the U.S. The U.S. claims that its security depends upon an agreement with Canada over the mineral wealth of North America, especially that in Canada. Canada refuses to enter into any pact, claiming that they do not know what their needs will be in twenty-five or fifty years and it would be foolish to make any arrangements which might hurt them in the future. (*New York Times,* May 31, 1970.)

The U.S. would like to include in the pact the use of Canadian fresh water for the arid Southwestern part of the U.S. Trudeau has made it very clear that Canadian water is not for sale. There has been a public outcry from Canadians to oppose letting "the Americans get our water." (*New York Times,* March 15, 1970.)

In response to this reduction in oil purchases, J. T. Greene, Minister of Energy, Mines and Resources, told a meeting of the Independent Petroleum Association that the U.S. must prepare for a much more nationalistic Canada "in which there will be control of all foreign investment, particularly in the resource industries." (*New York Times,* May 31, 1970.) Currently U.S. companies own or control about two-thirds of all oil and mineral production in Canada.

It was announced in 1970 that the U.S. had twenty-seven billion dollars of investments in Canada, two billion higher than in 1968. The total amount of foreign ownership for 1969 was also announced: 56.7% manufacturing, 82.6% oil and gas, 42% metal mining, 99.9% oil refining, 84.9% smelting. Most of the foreign ownership in Canada is American. (*New York Times,* June 22.) The Canadian government has begun to respond to this. The Roman Corporation, Ltd. of Toronto planned to sell 25.5% of the ownership in Denison Mines, Ltd. (a uranium mine) to the Hudson Bay Oil and Gas Co. which is owned by the Continental Oil Co. of New York. Trudeau, who has said that living next to the U.S. is like sleeping with an elephant, immediately went to Commons and said that the Government would even present legislation if necessary to prevent a foreign company from controlling a Canadian uranium mine. The government has limited foreign ownership of uranium mines to 33% and has discussed the possibility of extending this limitation to other industries. (*New York Times,* April 5, 1970.)

A blue-ribbon committee of financiers issued a report in June 1970 recommending that foreign companies be prevented from acquiring ownership in Canadian securities firms. Unlike in the U.S., where nationalist sentiments are frequently lodged in the political right, Canadian nationalism has been closely connected to the left. Such a surprising recommendation, coming from the "traditional champions of unfettered money movements," indicates a widening participation of the nationalist feelings within Canadian society.

To stem the cultural domination by their southern neighbor, the Canadian Radio-TV Commission has announced that all Canadian stations must increase the number of Canadian programs, thereby reducing American programming. (However, many Canadians are buying cable service which will bring them American stations; apparently nationalist considerations are of secondary importance when their TV habits are at stake!) (*New York Times,* April 5, 1970.) In the educational sphere, Canadians are protesting the prevalence of U.S. professors in the universities. Currently 75 percent of all new appointments are going to non-Canadians, most of whom are Americans. (*New York Times,* April 5, 1970.)

In addition to reducing the American presence in Canadian life, the government has seen in increased relations with other foreign nations a means toward strengthening Canadian independence. The June 1970 White Paper recommended an expansion of Canadian intercourse with Europe and the developing countries in Africa, Asia, and Latin America. Specifically, Canadian trade with Communist China and the pursuing of diplomatic relations with her to help that country "into a more constructive relationship with the world" reflect this independent stance. (*New York Times,* June 25, 1970.) (Since that White Paper Canada has extended diplomatic recognition to Communist China.)

J. T. Greene, Minister of Energy, Mines and Resources, in the speech cited earlier, made Canadian nationalism very explicit when he added that Canada wants to be herself and to avoid "the malaise that exists in your land." He cited the U.S. government's involvement in Southeast Asia, campus unrest, disorder in the streets, and problems of pollution as major reasons for Canada's desire "to be different." While some persons in the Canadian oil industry were unhappy with Greene's speech, his mail ran ten to one in favor of his nationalistic language. (*New York Times,* May 31, 1970.)

The emigration of American draft resisters and military deserters into Canada constitutes one more dynamic in U.S.-Canadian relations. By receiving these men, Canada is asserting her independence from her southern neighbor. In March, 1970, the Prime Minister told a delegation of Mennonites that Canada will continue to be a refuge from militarism. Washington has expressed official objection to Canadian policy, but the sincerity of that objection has been questioned. Some observers feel that the U.S. Government is not unhappy with Canada's acceptance of its dissidents; for the emigration of those men who strongly dislike the U.S. policy in Southeast Asia means that their voices will not be heard—at least through normal political processes.

Canada has not, however, offered U.S. draft age immigrants any special privileges. Resisters and deserters must go through the same immigration process as any immigrant, and no special help is offered to them once they are landed. By comparison, Canada did extend privileges to Hungarian immigrants in 1956 and to the Czechs in 1968. An immigration office was opened in Vienna after the occupation of Prague to help those Czechs interested in emigrating to Canada. Special assistance in job training and other benefits has been given to certain immigrant groups, but Americans are not included.

How far Canada is willing to go to assert her independence from the U.S. is still to be determined. Current friction between the two countries remains at the level of a lover's quarrel rather than a major division. Many Canadians would be anxious that their government not do anything which would bring repercussions more serious than the cutback in oil purchases.

THE EMIGRANT FACES
MANY RISKS ALONE

The deserter and the draft resister face many risks. There is the risk of getting caught, the risk of being rejected by family and friends, the risk of not being accepted by Canada, the risk of going to a new country where he has no friends, no place to stay, no promise of a job, and the risk of an open future where "making it" is up to the individual.

The last risk is particularly frightening. Changing countries means that his success or failure is up to him. His success at finding and holding a job will be up to his initiative and skill. His success at finding a wife and a community will depend upon his aggressiveness and ability to relate to new people. The help usually given by family, friends, school, church and other institutions by virtue of long association or birth will not be there. Emigrating is an act similar to a pioneer's move west—many of the same risks are involved.

Yet by risking a leap into an open future even a greater risk is taken. He risks being considered and considering himself less than a man. American society often links being a soldier with being a man. That same society equates manhood and success in a job. If the young man refuses to be a soldier and emigrates, thereby increasing the possibility of failure in a job, fears of not being a man can plague him. He leaves a society where being a strong, aggressive man is a virtue. He leaves at an age when being a "man" is very important to most men.

These are the risks of an emigrant. Most handle them well and are successful in their new country. A few are immobilized by the risks. Even after arriving in Canada the risks of an open future are so frightening that the man can become incapacitated. He doesn't seek work because he fears failing at holding or finding a job. He does not seek permanent housing or apply as a landed immigrant because the possibility of failing at these things is too frightening. By doing this he avoids the risk of blaming himself for the failure. Sometimes the immobilization for the emigrant takes the form of dependence on hard drugs or the development of severe emotional problems.

Though some men arriving in Canada are incapacitated by an understanding of themselves as less than a man, experiencing shame and guilt, many are able to reject the definition of manhood set down by their former society. They redefine manhood in terms of love, action, growth, openness and responsiveness.

However the risks are resolved, the man primarily faces them alone. When support exists for taking risks, then they become less threatening. The person who works his way through a university, the artist who takes creative leaps, the young man entering politics, are all taking risks—yet these are accepted by society as valuable and necessary and hence the person finds himself supported in the risk-taking.

The draft resister and deserter is not supported by society—neither the one he is leaving nor the one he is entering. The risks taken by the emigrant are not understood, appreciated, or supported by the dominant culture. Certainly there are persons in each society who are helpful and even a greater number are in agreement with his stand. The Aid Centers in Canada and many Canadians have helped many men. Yet the dominant society in the U.S. and Canada is hostile to his act. In the U.S. it is not thought that people should emigrate from the U.S.; they come *to* its shores. The Statue of Liberty welcomes immigrants, it does not bid farewell to emigrants. The implication is that the individual who feels he must emigrate must have something wrong with him. A *Life* magazine article on an Indiana family that emigrated to Canada because they found the U.S. a closed society, reported that many residents in their town sent hate mail condemning them.

A diversity of views exists among Canadians about U.S. draft age immigrants. The Canadian government's stand seems to reflect, among other things, their understanding of the skills and potential manpower resources that American draft age men bring. Many Canadians also understand that persons may find conscription to be morally wrong. Canada has no draft, and anti-militarism, especially in Quebec, is strong. Other Canadians take a laissez-faire attitude toward the men, saying that a person's background in his previous country (unless he committed a major crime) is of little consequence to his new life in Canada. A growing anti-Americanism, because of an extensive and expanding economic influence in Canada, often brings a welcome to those Americans who have left the country. A number of Canadians give direct aid to deserters and resisters. Canadians have played a significant role in the formation of Aid Centers.

On the other hand, the current high unemployment rate in Canada worries many that more Americans moving to their country will just make the job market tighter and will hurt them personally. The same anti-Americanism described above often has the effect of causing Canadians to look at deserters and resisters as one more extension of U.S. dominance in their country. Often Canadians are unhappy that American draft age immigrants have broken the law in their former country. Law-breaking of any kind is considered by many to be wrong and so these Americans are rejected. Also, many Canadians who fought in World War II or the Korean War find the concept of desertion abhorrent and do not want deserters of the U.S. Army, no matter what their reasons are in coming (the probable attitude of those immigration officials who discriminated against U.S. deserters).

Recently the mayor of Vancouver has spoken out against the hippies and draft dodgers, lumping the two together. This kind of thinking is becoming more popular as fear, distrust and even hatred of the youth culture continues to grow.

Therefore resisters and deserters do not find undisputed support, but ambivalence from the Canadian public at large. They take their risks in their new country alone. Their success or failure depends largely upon themselves.

THE EXODUS REFLECTS NEW
UNDERSTANDING OF REALITY

In the 1920's, Werner Heisenberg stated his now famous "Uncertainty Principle"—that it is impossible to tell the momentum and the location of an electron at the same time. The implication of this principle is that subjective factors and instrumental inadequacies necessarily influence perception—even in science, "the great objective discipline."

Thomas Kuhn's concept of "paradigm," developed in his book *The Structure of Scientific Revolutions* (Chicago: University of Chicago Press, 1962) is also helpful in understanding the thinking of men who emigrate to Canada. He defines a paradigm as a matrix of presuppositions, methodologies, and conceptions of reality which provides the scientist with a framework in which to work. The "truths" or "laws" discovered are products of the methodology, the instruments used, the expectations, and the understanding of reality as well as the phenomenon being studied.

In contrast to Heisenberg and Kuhn, a common understanding of reality is that truth is objective, discoverable and existent independent of man and his culture. This kind of thinking has its roots in the philosophy of Plato and has been reinforced by the great changes in technology of the last 50 years. In the field of aesthetics, religion and ethics, reality was similarly perceived. Values were understood as objective facts, realities with an independent existence. It was thought that they could be objectified and, using a scientific method, verified and substantiated. At least one professional school of philosophy attempted this task.

Thomas Kuhn brought his understanding of the dynamics of science one step further, however, indicating the times in the history of science when the paradigm in use becomes inadequate. Under those conditions, a new one takes its place. Galileo, Newton, and Einstein are names of scientists associated with paradigm change. The process of moving from one to another, as the new supercedes the old, has usually been marked by great struggle within the ranks of scientists.

One of the explosive dynamics within American society reflects the struggle of a philosophical and cultural "paradigm change." Many people—especially young people—consider an approach to values as objective and rigid realities nonsensical, that instead an approach similar to that of Heisenberg and Kuhn is most useful in approaching the dynamics of today's world. This is not radical subjectivity, which operates on the assumption that an individual should act according to his private values. The emerging approach to reality accepted by many young people states that values are the reflections of the biases and thoughts of a particular time and place. In rebellion against static and objectified values, youth are attempting to discover values by which they can live, and how those values will be manifested in their lives and in a more human social order.

Many men go to Canada in the belief that the dominant society in the U.S. will not permit them to experiment with new values, nor to live out the values they have already chosen. In defense of this view, they point to the draft as an example of an instrument which prevents experimentation with values. First, a man is forced to spend two years of his life in a very controlled environment. Second, the values of the Army are fixed and unchallengeable and are often dehumanizing. Many men also point to the schools, the courts and other institutions, emphasizing their rigidity and their refusal to permit openness toward new values and visions.

There have been many times in the history of the world when individuals or groups have come to believe that their nation prevents their values from being formed and lived out and so have left that nation. Religious and political groups in the seventeenth century left Europe and emigrated to America precisely because they believed that their culture was closed to their attempt to live their values. Many who emigrated in the Great Migration to America during the nineteenth century perceived their nation as a closed and rigid one. During that century the example of rigidity often pointed to as the reason for leaving was conscription. A large number of Americans today are descendants from draft dodgers and deserters who left nineteenth century Europe. Floods of persons have left Communist nations also because these refugees found that experimentation with new values or the living out of previously cherished values was impossible.

Along with rebellion against the belief in values as objectified and rigid realities is the disenchantment with the use of linear rationalism as a means of analysis and problem solving. Technology not only reinforced belief in values as objective reality, but confirmed the belief that rationalism of "the scientific method" was the most effective and efficient way to solve problems.

Here again, a look at a comparable paradigm change in physics may be helpful. For centuries Newton's laws of motion were adequate models of physical reality. But the motion of sub-atomic particles left scientists completely baffled as long as they retained their Newtonian perspective. Ultimately quantum theories were developed to better explain the apparently random behavior of the sub-atomic world.

Although striking the first of a row of billiard balls sets off an almost perfectly predictable, linear chain reaction, the behavior of a row of electrons is not so tidy. One sub-atomic "billiard ball" may hit another at a certain speed and force, but the second will not go on to hit the third. It may instead go out at a 90 degree angle or come back to hit the first. The particles will have random behavior that can only be understood through some model of probability.

The contention of many in the current youth generation is that the current dynamics in the world are more accurately explained and consequently problems are better solved by using a model closer to the quantum theory than to the Newtonian linear theory. A matrix—as is used in probability determinations—is sometimes suggested as a way to deal with the nuances and aesthetical and ethical qualities of life. Whichever model is used, many young people state that the rational, linear method is no longer useful.

Many parents try to dismiss what they see as a "generation gap" as something they "also had." What they fail to acknowledge, though they clearly feel it, is that there is a vast difference between their rebellion against their parents and their children's struggles against them. As one middle-aged parent put it, "We revolted strongly against our parents. But we were rebels for control of the system—it was basically a battle of power. We never bothered to go through the rejection symbols, the dress, the attitudes, and the development of a counter life style. We find our children revolting—and that's exactly what they are trying to say. They are revolting against many of the structured values in our style of life." (Colin W. Williams, Dean of the Divinity School, Yale University, in an address to the Department of Ministry, National Council of Churches, 1970.)

THIS EXODUS REQUIRES
A NEW UNDERSTANDING
OF CONSCIENCE

Selective Service System Form 150—the special form for men applying as conscientious objectors—makes several demands of the applicant. Among other things, it requires the man to explain how his claim that he cannot participate in war is based upon religious training and belief. (The Supreme Court has stated that the system of belief which holds the man's allegiance does not have to be religious, but can be ethical, philosophical, etc. Dr. Tarr, Director of Selective Service, has qualified the decision by saying that it cannot be just a personal code. The man's rationale for refusing to fight must be based on some system of belief which is held by a number of people and which has been taught to him.)

In this question in particular and in the entire Form 150, the Selective Service System makes three assumptions about the nature of conscience. First, it presupposes that the most appropriate way to solve problems such as whether to fight or not is through a rational, linear approach. According to this scheme a person is led to his conclusion by the force of rationality from his "system of belief."

As stated previously, many young people have rejected that kind of rationalism as an inaccurate and incomplete way to approach problems. Many considerations, including aesthetical and ethical ones as well as rational ones, lead to a decision about whether to kill or not. Many men find that the rational method is unable to dig out all of the many reasons and feelings they have for refusing to kill.

Second, the Selective Service System seems to also assume that the conscientious objector arrives at his conclusion because of a system of belief which he holds. Many young people today do not accept systems of belief, saying that the world is too complex and filled with too many ambiguities to be fit into any structured understanding of reality. The way values are worked out needs to be discovered in actual life situations. It is no longer possible to apply a system to specific instances because no system functions that well.

A third assumption made by Selective Service is that the conscientious objector should be able to articulate his belief clearly and well. In fact, articulation is often equated with sincerity. The only man ever to be granted a C.O. discharge from the U.S. Navy at the Annapolis Naval hospital was an articulate philosophy major from Johns Hopkins University.

Many young people find this kind of articulation false, claiming again that the beliefs concerning war are often too complex to be fit into neat concepts and well-formed phrases. They also state that it is impossible to know one's feelings so well that this kind of articulateness is possible. Describing one's feelings on war truthfully is going to require a description of ambivalent feelings and ambiguities, contradictory statements and uncertainties—a fact which does not usually produce articulateness.

Unfortunately, many other groups and individuals in our society accept the Selective Service definition of conscience. Many on the Right and the Left think that a system of belief, a rational approach and articulateness are necessary "proofs" for the sincere conscientious objector. The man who seems to contradict himself or who spends a great deal of time explaining certain ambiguities does not seem to be sincere.

There are some deserters and resisters in Canada who are very articulate and appear to have approached the decision of their emigration in a very rational fashion; others hold a system of belief which has led to this conclusion—there are a number of very religious draft resisters and deserters. However, many men in Canada are inarticulate, reject rationalism and have no system or belief. They state simply that the war in Vietnam is wrong, or the Army is brutal to both its enemies and to its own soldiers or that the United States is a closed country and that they do not want to live there anymore.

These statements are from the gut and come from many hours

of struggling. It is also true that this struggling will go on after they cross into Canada. Their emigration was a visceral response to certain situations—in most cases, orders to go to Vietnam. Once arrived in Canada, the men continue struggling with the "why" of their actions.

The men in Canada can be called men of conscience. But their conscience is not the static conclusion of an ideology which is required by the Selective Service System and others. Conscience is a process. Conscience is a process of dealing with a visceral reaction. Conscience is a process of discovering something is wrong, trying to discover what it is and how it can be rectified. Conscience is the process of trying to understand how to work for a better world.

The unfortunate thing about the men in Canada is that most have recently entered the process of conscience and now the choice they were forced to make has required them to continue that process in an atmosphere of uncertainty and risk. Perhaps the process of conscience always requires risk-taking. Yet it is sad that men are forced to deal early in their process of conscience with such ultimately important and dangerous decisions.

THE FUTURE OF THE EXODUS

Two descriptions of the emigration of draft age men from the United States to Canada are "exile" and "exodus." Exodus in the biblical sense means a going forth and connotes a permanent exit. As there was an exodus of the ancient Hebrews from Egypt, so young Americans are leaving their country, never to return.

An exile, on the other hand, not only is forced to leave his country, but longs to go back. The Israelites understood their forced exile as a temporary sojourn from which they would return as soon as circumstances permitted. ". . . I will restore your fortunes and gather you from all the nations and all the places I have driven you, says the Lord, and I will bring you back to the place from which I sent you into exile" (Jer. 29:14). This feeling does not dominate the draft age men in Canada. While concern exists for the United States, the majority have come to Canada to make it their home. Perhaps hardest for parents and friends to understand is that their children in Canada have made the decision to leave permanently. Except for the fact that they will be unable to visit family and friends back home, few express regret over being unable to return to the United States.

The question of amnesty has been raised in response to this inability of resisters and deserters to re-enter the United States without prosecution. Several Americans have pointed out what a proclamation of amnesty would mean not only to the recipients of this gesture but for the United States' national life. The late Richard Cardinal Cushing in his 1970 Easter sermon suggested this in part: "Would it be too much to suggest that this Easter we . . . call back from over the border and around the world the young men who are called deserters? Perhaps this year we should dramatize this notion of beginning, of newness, by doing something unprecedented in our life as a nation." Dr. John Swomley, Professor of Christian Ethics at St. Paul School of Theology, has written an article entitled: "Memo to Nixon: Why Not An Amnesty?" In discussing his position that amnesty would be essential for the U.S. national health, Swomley states:

> "One major purpose of amnesty is to heal the wounds and divisions of war, to restore confidence in government on the part of those who have been alienated by the war. It is obvious that the former Presidents of the United States who declared amnesty during the armed uprisings in the 1790's and the 1860's had such healing in mind. The division in the United States today is just as real. It is not based on sectional grievances, nor is it confined to any part of the United States. Rather it is chiefly defined by age or by the kind of idealism that expected the United States to behave differently from other nations. There has been a loss of faith in the government of the United States by thousands of Americans. An act of amnesty now would go a long way toward restoration of faith of young Americans in their government.
>
> Amnesty by any government is generally a sign of governmental strength and always a sign of magnanimity. The

Encyclopedia of the Social Sciences says that 'the granting of an anmesty is nearly always a sign that the government feels its position secure and that having disarmed its enemy in the field, it may proceed with the attempt at disarming hatred and resentment by an act of grace.' Since modern limited wars seldom end in victory for either side, amnesty for those who refused to participate in the war would be an even greater indication of the security of the government that proclaims it." (*National Catholic Reporter,* Jan. 1, 1969.)

From the perspective of most draft age immigrants in Canada, however, amnesty appears neither relevant nor a concern of high priority. Roger Williams, a draft resister, indicated in an article in *The New Republic* that such a general pardon by the U.S. government would not in fact be a viable act: "Unity comes on the question of amnesty. No one wants it, though reasons for disparaging the idea differ. Individuals and groups concerned primarily with bringing the young refugees into Canadian life, making sure they are an asset and not a political liability, know that to discuss amnesty or work for it is to impinge on the welcome here— 'What? Isn't Canada good enough for you?'—and to psychologically disorient the newcomer, distracting him from taking Canada and his new life seriously. Likewise, the politicized, the radicals who *do* want to go back, or who think of themselves *only* as temporary residents, are insulted by the very discussion of amnesty. The analogy to Nazi Germany is drawn: Willy Brandt didn't ask for, nor would have accepted, amnesty from the Third Reich, and yet his civil rights as a German citizen were eventually restored as were those of thousands of others. Amnesty implies guilt, they say, and they do not feel guilty." (*The New Republic,* "The New Exodus," Washington, D.C., Vol. 162, No. 20, May 16, 1970, p. 16.) Said one young deserter: "Amnesty is your problem. I feel what I have done was right, and that the United States is wrong. Why should I ask for amnesty?" Few emigrants to Canada indicate any desire to return permanently to the U.S.

Another response to the crisis of conscience among draft age men attempts to broaden the Selective Service criteria regarding conscientious objection to include men of conscience who will not fight in particular wars—such as the war in Vietnam.

Congressman Edward Koch, one of the earliest congressional leaders sensitive to this dilemma, asked the Congress and the President in early 1969 to redefine conscientious objection to include selective objection to particular wars based on conscience and to allow those in jail, in the military, or residing in another country to apply for it. Pointing out that his proposal was not a call for a general amnesty, he presented H.R. 10501 to the House on April 23, 1969 as a "second chance": "I am introducing a bill today that would provide a second chance to those young men who have been opposed to participation in the Vietnam war and yet have been forced into the heartrending dilemma of service in a war they oppose or prison or flight from the country. By second chance, I mean giving a young man the opportunity now to offer information to his local board in substantiation of his claim to exemption from military service, provided he was conscientiously opposed to participation in a particular war at the time he received a notice to report for induction or at the time he left a jurisdiction to evade military service." (*Congressional Record,* April 23, 1969, p. H3004.)

Mr. Koch's bill was referred to the Committee on Armed Services.

As has been emphasized, many young emigrants perceive the war in Southeast Asia and the draft as only indications of the rigidness and lack of openness of American society. The exodus is not only a "no" to its military policies in Southeast Asia, but it is a "no" to the quality of life and the style of the United States generally. For these reasons the exodus will probably continue, even if the war and the draft should end.

Not only have draft age men made the decision to leave the U.S. Many adults who are not draft age, nor in the armed forces, have made that choice as well. The July 17, 1970 issue of *Life* told the story of one of many families which has emigrated to Canada. The father, a very successful businessman, explained their move: "Our society is inflexible. It's grown old." After being in Canada for two months he concluded: "We find the Canadians more oriented to people and their needs, and less to a system."

The United States, which for so long had been the receiver of immigrants discontented with their native land and looking for new hope has now become a large source of emigrants. In 1969, 22,785 Americans emigrated to Canada, while 3,418 left for Australia. Canadian officials estimate that the 1969 figure will go up by at least a third in 1970, and Australian officials expect an even more dramatic increase than that. There is an increasing number of American Jews who are moving to Israel permanently. Among the various motives leading people to make this exodus, dissatisfaction with the United States plays a major role.

A recent survey by the Australian government indicates that U.S. immigrants, in contrast to every other group that came to Australia since World War II, left "just to get away." (*New York Times,* Aug. 23, 1970, p. 12.)

chapter 9
EPILOGUE:
A MAN WITHOUT
A COUNTRY

Black Soldier's Burial Is Held Up in Florida

FORT PIERCE, Fla., Aug. 23 (AP)—A soldier killed in Vietnam, who was rejected by a cemetery because he was black, was given military and religious honors at an armory today and then carried to a mortuary.

Willis Edwards, a black student from Los Angeles who delivered the eulogy, called the 20-year-old soldier, Specialist 4 Pondexteur Eugene Williams, "a man without a country."

In his eulogy, Mr. Edwards told the soldier's parents, "I am sorry that a man fought for his country and his family has to go through the extra pain of waiting for a court order to bury your son because he doesn't have six feet of U.S. ground to lay his head."

Hillcrest Memorial Gardens had refused to allow the burial in a grave donated to the soldier's family by a 72-year-old white woman. A Federal court in Miami will be asked tomorrow to order the burial in the all-white cemetery.

(*New York Times,* Sunday August 23, 1970)

"All I want to ask the United States is to be true to itself. Until that time, it denies itself in the worst possible way, and many others of us will search for new countries." So claimed a young resister in explaining why he had left the U.S. "What I was taught to believe about the U.S. just does not exist, perhaps it never will, perhaps it never did."

The forces and values that led these young men to flee their homes and country were not created in a vacuum; they have roots and history in the American experience. Nowhere could the young have learned the lesson of oppression and rebellion so well as from their history books. The U.S. was a nation formed because of rebellion against perceived oppression, because a people wanted to be free of an outside power—criticisms of oppression and aggressive domination made about the U.S. by many young people today.

Young people are taught the virtues of justice, human dignity, self-determination, and love by their parents and culture. But they have found in those teachers a rejection in practice of those very virtues, and the response of many has been to reject the teachers in order to practice the virtues they have taught.

In the rebellion against parents and nation, there is frequently a feeling, articulated or not, that that which the young rebel is against is his origin and creators. While youth can rebel, they can neither leave nor ignore the influences that formed them. In fact, not only do the young remain under the influence of their origin, but there is often love for that origin, for their roots.

Men who have emigrated to Canada often have love and respect for pater and patria. Their nation and parents nurtured them in the values which led to their decision. In practical terms, most young men have experienced great anxiety in making the choice to cross the border and reside in Canada. Tension between rebellion and love generates anguish, guilt, loneliness, and immense feelings of inadequacy. Emigration requires a man to deal with tension in an atmosphere of intense immediacy and power. In taking the ultimate act of rebellion—leaving parents and nation—they test the balance between love and rejection in an extreme way.

Yet Canada has given to these young men more than another chance. It has given them hope, enabling them to channel their rebellion into creative new outlets. Canada has done something for a significant group of Americans that the United States itself could not do.

APPENDIX A
THE NUMBER OF U.S. DRAFT AGE
EMIGRANTS IN CANADA

The Canadian government does not keep a record of the number of U.S. deserters and resisters: immigration officers are not permitted to note a man's military status on his record. It is impossible to tell with any certainty the motivation of men immigrating to Canada. However, there are several factors which give an indication of the number of U.S. draft age immigrants in Canada.

1. THE NUMBER OF DESERTERS. In fiscal 1970 there were 89,088 deserters—men who are absent without leave for 30 days or more. The Department of Defense does not release the number of men who return. Assuming that 90% do go back (a rather high estimate), about 8,900 men in fiscal 1969 alone have left the Army permanently.

2. THE REPORT OF THE AID CENTERS. During the summer and fall of 1969, most Aid Centers in Canada reported receiving a large increase in the numbers of deserters and resisters, with some groups, including the Toronto Anti-Draft Programme (the largest group in Canada) reporting a double case load. Yet there are two problems here. Not all the groups keep permanent records and some deserters and resisters do not inform the Aid Centers as to the final disposition of their case.

During the summer of 1970, all Aid Centers experienced great increases in the number of men. In Vancouver during March, 1970, 15 men a week were going to the Vancouver Committee to Aid War Resisters. During the summer of that year 75 men a week were seen. In Montreal 20 men a week were interviewed in March, 1970 while 15 a day were helped during that summer.

3. NUMBER OF AMERICAN STUDENTS. There has been a 61% rise in the number of American students (male and female) attending Canadian universities from 1965 through 1969. The figures for those years were:

1965	4,742
1966	6,661
1967	7,386
1968	7,679
1969	7,674

4. THE NUMBERS OF DRAFT AGE AMERICAN MALES RECEIVING LANDED IMMIGRANT STATUS.

Year	Age Group	No. of Immigrants	Total That Year
1965	18-19	155	
	20-24	696	
	25-29	916	1,767
1966	18-19	239	
	20-24	910	
	25-29	1,059	2,208
1967	18-19	291	
	20-24	1,233	
	25-29	1,218	2,742
1968	18-19	310	
	20-24	1,999	
	25-29	1,457	3,766
1969	18-19	343	
	20-24	2,175	
	25-29	1,584	4,102
1970			2,051
		Total for 5½ Years	16,636*

*A. The number in the 18-19 age bracket is found by dividing the Immigration Department figures for the 15-19 age group by one-half. It is assumed that the largest number of men in the 15-19 group would be in the 18-19 bracket.

B. Even though men over the age of 26 are not normally liable for the draft, the entire 25-29 age bracket is included for the following reasons:

1. A large number of deserters over the age of 26 emigrate to Canada.

2. A large number of young men emigrate to Canada in response to what they see as a closed and rigid America. Many of these men are not facing threat of induction.

3. Men between the ages of 26 and 35 who have had a deferment and have not been drafted are liable for the draft in times of national emergency when there is a great need for manpower.

C. The figure for the first half of 1970 was found by dividing the number for 1969 by one-half. This results in a very conservative figure since it does not take into consideration the increase that has occurred each year in this age bracket. This figure also does not take into account the very large increase of men who visited the Aid Centers in 1969 and 1970. The figures from the Immigration Department only include men who have received their final papers as landed immigrants—a process which normally takes four months from the time he is first told that he has been landed. Therefore a man who receives his first landed paper in October, 1969 will not be in the statistics until 1970. We also recognize that not all men in the draft age bracket had an order for induction or were in the military. We believe, however, that the overwhelming majority were in the military and that the others can find a haven from the draft, whether that was their primary motivation or not.

We claim therefore that there are at least 30,000 U.S. draft age immigrants in Canada: a conservative estimate, since the figure includes not only those who are actually landed, but those who are waiting for final landed papers, students, and men in

Canada illegally. It should be remembered that the Aid Centers report large increases in the number of deserters and resisters who have sought their help in 1969 and 1970.

It is also interesting to note the constant rise of U.S. immigrants to Canada while both the total number of immigrants and those from Great Britain, the largest source, continued to fluctuate.

1963	Total	93,151
	Britain and Ireland	25,193
	Italy	14,427
	U.S.	11,736
1964	Total	112,565
	Britain and Ireland	29,959
	Italy	19,297
	U.S.	12,565
1965	Total	146,758
	Britain and Ireland	40,718
	Italy	26,378
	U.S.	15,143
1966	Total	194,743
	Britain and Ireland	65,065
	Italy	31,625
	U.S.	17,514
1967	Total	222,876
	Britain and Ireland	64,601
	Italy	30,055
	U.S.	19,038
1968	Total	183,974
	Britain and Ireland	39,434
	Italy	20,422
	U.S.	19,774
1969	Total	161,531
	Britain and Ireland	33,212
	Italy	10,383
	U.S.	22,785

It is difficult to explain such a large increase in the number of Americans emigrating to Canada. Economic opportunities and job transferrals certainly play a large role. However, the increase probably does contain a large number of persons of all ages discontented with their country.

It is interesting to note that the number of Canadians immigrating to the United States has decreased drastically. The change brought about by the 1965 immigration law, that affected quotas previously in force, contributes to this decrease, but other factors were certainly at work. In 1965 there were 40,013 immigrants from Canada. In fiscal 1970, there were 12,263.

APPENDIX B
AID CENTERS IN CANADA

VICTORIA
Victoria Committee to Aid Draft Resisters
Fred Johnson
1132 Goodwin Street
Victoria, B.C.
Phone: 604/388-6939

VANCOUVER
Vancouver Committee to Aid War Objectors
Box 4321
Vancouver 9, British Columbia
Phone: 604/255-1918

CALGARY
Calgary Committee for War Immigrants
Box 3234 Station B
Calgary, Alberta
Phone: 403/245-4006; 265-7540

EDMONTON
Alexander Ross Society
Roy Swift
4703–105 "A" Street

Edmonton, Alberta
Phone: 403/439-7198

SASKATOON
Saskatoon Immigrant and Refugee Aid Society
c/o Rev. Andree Poilievre
St. Michael Rectory
1228 Idylwyld Drive North
Saskatoon, Saskatchewan
Phone: 306/244-6711

REGINA
Dr. Dallas Smythe
4336 Castle Road
Regina, Saskatchewan
Phone: 306/536-3607

WINNIPEG
Winnipeg Committee to Assist War Objectors
All Saints Anglican Church
175 Colony Street
Winnipeg 9, Manitoba
Phone: 204/533-8793; 475-6667

NEW BRUNSWICK
Anti-Draft Programme
Apt. 3/11 Prince William St.
Saint John, New Brunswick
Phone: 506/657-1149

LONDON
London Aid for Draft Refugees
1542 Western Road
c/o K. Roberts
London 72, Ontario
Phone: 519/434-2372; 434-6362

HALIFAX
Nova Scotia Committee to Aid American War Objectors
P.O. Box 19
Armdale, Nova Scotia

HAMILTON
Southern Ontario Committee on War Immigrants
Box 155, Station E
Hamilton, Ontario

KITCHENER-WATERLOO
Ronald Lambert
410 Meadowbrook Drive
Kitchener, Ontario
Phone: 519/576-5267

OTTAWA
Assistance with Immigration and Draft
Box 2382, Station D
Ottawa, Ontario
Phone: 613/236-3933

THUNDER BAY
Lakehead Committee to Aid American War Objectors
98 Peter Street
Thunder Bay, Ontario
Phone: 807/344-8559

TORONTO
Anti-Draft Programme
Box 41, Station K
Toronto, Ontario
Phone: 416/481-0241

Committee to Aid Refugees from Militarism
P. O. Box 5627, Station "A"

Toronto, Ontario
Phone: 416/922-3373

The Hall
19 Huron Street
Toronto, Ontario
Phone: 416/863-0275

MONTREAL
Council to Aid War Resisters
Box 5
Montreal, Quebec
Phone: 514/843-3132

Carbie St. Louis Hostel
3615 St. Urbaine
Montreal, Quebec
Phone: 514/843-8571

Montreal American Counselling Service
3971 St. Denis
Montreal, Quebec
Phone: 514/844-3126